Rapid Implementation

Rapid Implementation

How to Complete a Low-cost and Successful Business Management System Implementation

It's not Rocket Science

Gloria J. Braunschweig, CMA

Dorian Moon Press LLC

Dorian Moon Press, LLC

Rapid Implementation

How to complete a low-cost successful business management system implementation

It's not Rocket Science

Gloria J. Braunschweig, CMA

Cover Design: Karyn Servin

Copyeditor: Lara Foote

Copyright © 2013 by Gloria J. Braunschweig, CMA

All Rights Reserved

This book was published by Dorian Moon Press, LLC. No part of this book may be reproduced in any form by any means without the express written permission of the author. This includes reprints, excerpts, photocopies, recording, or any future means of reproducing text.

If you would like to do any of the above, please seek permission first by contacting me at www.rapidimplementation.com.

Published in the United States by Dorian Moon Press, LLC

ISBN 978-1-4675-5529-6

Dedicated to my daughters, Lara and Emily,

and to Rob Lloyd, a friend for life

Table of Contents

Acknowledgements vii
Acronyms, Definitions, and Copyrights viii
Introduction xi
Overview xv
I. Change the Outcome by Changing Your Management Support 1
II. Rapid Selection of Software 13
III. Get Your Ducks in a Row 33
IV. A Firm's Rapid Implementation Success 39
V. KISS Project Management for Dragon Slayers 45
VI. Rocket Through the Clouds 53
VII. Software Licensing 70
VIII. Swim with Your Software Vendor without Getting Stung 71
IX. A Square Egg 85
X. Other Assessments to Make 93
XI. Enabling Rapid or Low-cost Implementation Through Prioritization 96
XII. Count Your Eggs Before They Hatch 104
XIII. Needs Analysis 111
XIV. Rapid Process Workflow Inside the Prototype 118
XV. The Right Tools 121
XVI. I'm Taking a Stand: The Egg Came First 128
XVII. Teaching the Chicks a New Trick 131
XVIII. Preparation of Master Records 139
XIX. Importing Historical Data 143
XX. Rapid Implementation Settings Unique to Microsoft Dynamics® GP 156
XXI. Document and Forms Formatting 159
XXII. Rapid Implementation of Financial Statements 162
XXIII. Support for Chicken Feed 164
XXIV. Working with Independent Software Vendors 168
XXV. Roasted Chicken—Yummy! 172
XXVI. Don't let the Fox in the Hen House 179
XXVII. Move Away from Custom Core Systems 188
XXVIII. A Rotten Egg 190
About the Author 194

Acknowledgements

Steve Bell, for motivating me to get started before the project became a rapid project.

Todd C. Williams, for priceless help to turn this idea into a rapid, agile project.

Jay Manley, for his motivation and feedback, and the vital information on RapidStart for Microsoft Dynamics GP.

Kim Peterson, for her help getting the book into the Convergence 2013 bookstore.

Mike Williams, for being my first client, a client since then multiple times, and a dear friend.

John Arnold, for being the most helpful volunteer editor a person could find.

Jason Gumpert, for his assistance with my blogs and critical feedback on this book.

Karyn Servin, for her art and thoughtful homage to Dorian Moon.

Lara Foote, because she stepped in as copyeditor when I needed the most help.

The Personnel at Computeration, for their boundless technical and personal support.

Acronyms, Definitions, and Copyrights

I passionately hate acronyms, but they are contained in the book when I think they're a universal term that nearly all readers will consistently understand or the phrase is just too darn long to keep typing or reading it over and over. I also believe it's more readable to put the acronym first then explain what it means. A glossary of acronyms and other several major definitions:

Agile	A flexible project with changes based on new information
AP	Accounts Payable
AR	Accounts Receivable
Blue-chip	Fortune 500 companies or ones of similar size and reputation
CRM/ARM	Customer Relationship Management which has morphed into any kind of Relationship Management
DIY	Do-it-Yourself
ERP	Enterprise Resource Planning
GL	General Ledger
Go Live	What is commonly called the day of activating the new system
GPIM	GP Integration Manager
HR/PR	Human Resources and Payroll
IT	Information Technology
Lean	Lean Practices are explained at http://www.lean.org/WhatsLean/
ODBC	Open Database Connectivity
RFI	Request for Information
RFP	Request for Proposal
RFQ	Request for Quote
SMB	Small and Mid-size Business (also known as Small and Medium-sized Business)
Sprint	A short, rapid stage of a project designed to focus the team on a specific task
VAR	Value-added Reseller
VB	Visual Basic
VBA	Visual Basic for Applications
WIP	Work in process

Mid-market Software Products

The business management system market is divided into big, medium, and small companies—tier one, mid-market, and entry level, respectively. I've worked with companies at all levels, but most of the material in this book is directed to mid-market companies. My examples cover multiple products, but I've been a Microsoft Dynamics® GP partner since 2003 and a Great Plains Software partner before that since 1990, so most technical material is directed exclusively towards Dynamics GP.

Dynamics GP is now one of four business management software products owned by Microsoft in their line of ERP (Enterprise Resource Planning) products in addition to a point of sale product and a customer relationship management product. The product line formally and legally is:

- Microsoft Dynamics® AX
- Microsoft Dynamics® CRM
- Microsoft Dynamics® GP
- Microsoft Dynamics® NAV
- Microsoft Dynamics® POS
- Microsoft Dynamics® SL

In addition, other products mentioned in the book include:

- Intuit QuickBooks®
- Sage 500 ERP®
- Sage 100 ERP®
- Sage X3®
- Peachtree® / Sage 50 Accounting®
- Oracle Fusion®

Trademarks, Copyrights, and Registration Marks

All trademarks, copyrights, and registered trademarks are the property of their respective owners.

Silver Bullets, Otherwise Known as Citations

Steven C. Bell, www.leanitstrategies.com

Gloria J. Braunschweig, www.computeration.com

Todd C. Williams, www.ecaminc.com

Introduction

Small and mid-size businesses need rapid, low-cost, successful implementations. It's time to help them achieve all three goals. Implementers always start with good intentions whether they're professional consultants or company personnel. Then the process starts to break down because of lack of resources or experience. In some cases, the breakdown occurs because of unwarranted optimism. For those instances, I've kept a magic wand in my office for many years.

SMBs (Small and Mid-size Businesses) and consultants are implementing at a time where competition is formidable. Even one-person companies are selling their products around the world. I fell in love with an Alpaca jacket last summer created by a woman in Peru who was regularly placing items on consignment in a Washington retail store.

New web stores are launching daily for owners who demand flexibility and integration. SMB owners survived Y2K, the dot.com bust, 9/11/2001, and the world-wide economic recession that started in 2008—the recession that we may be recovering from even though many companies and people haven't regained the economic position they had achieved in 2007. Flexibility, accuracy, and rapid implementation are vital to the companies creating jobs and aiding the economic recovery.

I've installed systems for companies which have prospered more than 50 years yet they have chosen or been forced to undergo major changes. Some companies are startups in the new digital economy. Outcomes I discuss in this book range from highly successful and rapid, through many mixed results, to the failures demonstrating the challenges from which we learn.

Most SMBs struggle with their implementations because of funding and resource limitations; I know that's a common problem with implementations because a number of times in my history as a reseller, I have heard statistics that indicate our Dynamics GP customer base is right at the average. The first statistics of that nature were expressed by an executive of Great Plains Software at a partner meeting in the early 1990's.

The statistics involved the average number of sales per year and the license value of those sales. The incident sticks in my memory because the executive had responded to another partner's question at the same conference, stating that privately-held Great Plains Software didn't announce revenue publicly. I overheard a lot of speculation in the next few days among many partners. I returned home, looked up my first and last invoices of the year, subtracted the number to find the total invoices, averaged the costs on the invoices, and multiplied. The next year in a short conversation with the executive, the topic arose again. I told him my guess; then I calmed him down by telling him no one had leaked the number. I told him how I had estimated it. Quite obviously from his reaction, my method was accurate, and I also confirmed I was an average reseller at that time.

Microsoft has also provided information to the partner channel over the years about the average Dynamics GP license value, so I theorize our clients aren't unique in their struggles. An underlying cause is that the same amount of basic training is needed whether we're training two employees or twelve, so the cost of implementation services are disproportionately high for SMBs.

This book is written for business owners, managers, and technology personnel. Most of the book addresses project culture—recommendations for the business owners and managers contemplating or involved in a business management system implementation. The remainder of the book addresses more technical decisions and processes that can be undertaken for a rapid implementation. I've added the last two chapters because I needed to write those stories down and stop telling them to anyone whom I could corner long enough to listen.

This book doesn't develop an entirely new approach of project management. It relies upon components of common project management theories. It also suggests that many common project management processes may be set aside. For that, I'm sure I'll take some criticism.

For mid-size companies—any with complex processes like manufacturing, project accounting, or not-for-profit management—more complex project management is warranted. The Microsoft Sure Step project management system proposes picking what's relevant from a long list of comprehensive processes. However, it occurred to me while working with various project management philosophies that the list of processes and documents would dissuade many SMBs from implementing mid-market products. Without exception in SMB implementations, the decision makers always ask how to cut costs.

My client list follows the 80/20 rule, the Pareto principle. 80% are companies under $50,000,000 in revenue and under 50 employees. 20% of our clients range from $50,000,000 to $750,000,000. This book is primarily written for the 80%, but with so many rapid and effective tips, I hope every reader can find something of assistance.

Rapid Implementation will mean many things to different people. I perceive that many SMB owners will equate a rapid implementation with a low-cost, do-it-yourself approach. I'll specifically address this approach in the book. Other readers are seeking a rapid implementation and recognize it can only be completed with a team of personnel and professional consultants.

Many SMB owners or managers will want to use the "silver bullet" approach with professional consultants only when they're stuck on a challenge they can't see past. Hopefully, they also will realize when they might get stuck and call before that point. These business owners optimize the use of their personnel for the bulk of the tasks, calling upon the consultants for the technical heavy lifting.

For young consultants, I hope to provide you with some tips and tricks to accelerate your implementations and become a silver bullet.

For all readers, the book strives to assist you with tools and methods to decrease the amount of time spent on implementations yet insure the implementation is successful. For all rapid implementations, the sooner you start using a new, powerful business management system, the more successful your implementation result, and the sooner you reap the benefits.

Case Studies and I, We, and You

Having taken a fair amount of criticism already about the use of "I, We, and You," I'll explain my position.

I'll bare my business soul and disguise the names, locations, and industries of my clients in order to use those examples to attempt to improve implementations about to be undertaken. All examples in this book are from my personal experiences, but I've distorted irrelevant characteristics to disguise the companies. I've omitted identification of the companies so my prospects and clients can remain anonymous and allow me to live with mobility and adequate retirement funds to an old age. For clarity with longer case studies, I'll add a descriptive adjective for the company name.

In the case studies, some of my clients will be able to identify themselves. It's hard to disguise some events. I hope that you can chuckle with me if you read my book and think, "She's writing about me." I'm sorry if my story makes you wince. I'll go with the cliché that I will neither confirm nor deny those events associated with your identity.

The book may seem randomly scattered with both "I" and "We." Over my decades of experience, I either worked alone, in internal implementation teams, or with teams of consultants. To accurately reflect the events and the fact that I have led a team of consultants for a number of years, I found I had to switch between "I" and "We" to make sense in the various scenarios. And I use "You" because I want you to take my recommendations to heart.

I concentrate on the effective and ineffective actions during implementations so that you can perhaps recognize yourself in the ineffective actions and change your process. Or you can envision yourself taking the effective actions that I point out in order to make your business management system implementation meet your goals. I've also flavored the book, sometimes with irrelevant material that I simply couldn't discard, to keep you entertained and awake. My goal is to make one more SMB more productive and profitable by making their implementation more successful—your implementation.

Overview

I perceive that there are seven important aspects of a rapid implementation. That's less than most project managers would include, but my point is that if you don't complete these, little else matters:

1. Effective management support
    a. Support and supply adequate resources
    b. Insightful assessment of your personnel
    c. Insightful assessment of your situation
2. Effective project management
3. Select the right people and provide them with adequate time
4. Engage with experienced consultants
5. Invest in training that meets your needs
6. Design and Prototype (more later on why I recommend a combination of these steps for a rapid implementation for some SMBs)
7. Configuration, integration, and implementation tools and techniques

Case Study: Rapid, Low-cost, Successful Implementation

With this ideal implementation, the client personnel were determined to do as much as possible on their own. With their previous system, consultants had designed and implemented it then taught the client personnel how to use the software. The employees felt that type of approach led to a lot of frustration and prolonged self-discovery of the system after the consultants were gone.

The team leader was insistent they would use their own documentation and processes for project management, including preparation of training videos with a prototype of their data. I estimate they cut their outside consultant costs in half and this was one of the most successful self-driven implementations in which I've participated.

There were three members on the core team with different areas of expertise: an accounting person who also acted as the project manager, an IT manager, and a quality control manager. They were supplemented by the manufacturing manager as needed.

Starting at the top down, the owner of the company fully supported the decision through an executive vice president who was general manager and chief operating officer. I met the general manager from time to time, often enough to see that he had an open door policy with the project team and fully supported their decisions.

The IT manager self-installed the software, creating both a prototype and live company database. He utilized our SQL database manager to review his implementation and from time to time consulted with our developer and integration specialist.

Cleaning legacy data was the primary responsibility of the IT manager. He completed the integration of nearly all the data and was assisted by our manufacturing specialist with bills of material and routings.

The project team didn't have temporary help during the implementation which stretched across four to six months. They worked in sprints of sixty and eighty hour weeks and were prepared for this type of schedule more so than most other teams with whom I've worked.

The team met with me and one other consultant weekly, primarily reviewing set up options in the system, especially in the manufacturing modules. They deferred set up of advanced modules until six months after the Go Live.

Recently I spent an hour on-line assisting the controller with a variety of questions. She moved as rapidly through the system as I do; in fact, there were times when I asked her to slow down so I could see click-by-click what she was doing.

These personnel own their system in the deepest sense, and I predict will successfully use it for years. They've added multiple third-party products and customizations to their system. They've attended the Microsoft Convergence conference two years in a row and participate in the annual GP Users Group conference and local GPUG meetings. My best wishes to them.

I. Change the Outcome by Changing Your Management Support

What you'll learn in this chapter
- *Three companies; right and wrong examples*
- *20 tips to make management support effective*

Dear Executive:

You are the most important person for your implementation project. Of all the deadly sins that can be committed and will be reported on in this book, you have the most influence over them. You provide your hard-earned equity, manage the personnel who will complete your implementation, and make the final decisions about hardware, licensing, training, and support.

Read any book or whitepaper on IT project management; read news articles about IT project failures and cost overruns; read case studies about implementation project successes—you will realize you are the primary deciding factor for success or failure. This book and the cases within it are your lessons.

Case Study: Effective Company

In March 2000, I was working alone at the time and was leaving my office for several days off, noting that I had worked seventeen months without a day off because of the Y2K date problem. The phone rang and I hesitated for several moments pondering whether to answer it. I was contacted by an individual with a company that had failed with its implementation which was to have been completed just prior to 12/31/1999. If you're older than a teenager, you probably remember that many legacy systems were unable to handle a date after 12/31/1999—the Y2K date problem causing many of us to sock away a fair amount of booze, cigarettes, toilet paper and food (all better tender than cash in a crisis) because surely the technical world would fall apart on 1/1/2000.

Because of the implementation failure, Effective Company replaced its controller, IT manager, and purchasing manager. The entity was about to sue their reseller when they were referred to me by a temporary employee who overheard the conversation about the lawsuit while she was being interviewed for a contract position.

As the controller related the story to me, the temp heard them state that they had been told there was only one Dynamics/eEnterprise installer in Oregon. She said that she knew of another; her name was Gloria; she knew nothing else. Taking a round-about path, they called Great Plains Software's technical support and asked the technician if he knew of an installer in Oregon named Gloria. Whomever that technician was, thank you.

The problem as I understood it: The purchasing manager had negotiated a fixed bid implementation with a fifteen percent discount against the software. The reseller had written a letter promising that the entity could complete its own implementation after the reseller had provided forty hours of training.

Once the training was complete, the staff realized they were unable to proceed on their own. While the reseller was willing to provide additional consulting resources, the client personnel speculated the rates were increased in order to make up for the software discount, and the relationship fell apart.

Realizing a sticky situation, I met first with the new controller and IT manager. Fortunately, the new IT manager was an experienced project manager, and the three of us put together a plan. The new IT manager already had a process in place for effective project management and the team was backed by effective management support.

Effective Management Support

- The CEO and CFO attended kick off meetings for all major projects
- The controller and IT manager held weekly status meetings with the CEO and CFO on all projects
- The core project team met weekly
- The core project team was held accountable with communicating to the users reporting to them—fifty-five stakeholders in total.

Effective Project Team Tactics

- I proposed a two-month implementation quote that had twenty percent contingency fees built in.
- The IT manager didn't know I built in a twenty percent contingency so he built in another twenty percent.
- I created a Gantt chart of twenty pages which the controller taped together and put on the wall in the finance office.
- We went live on target and under my twenty percent contingency proposal which involved 200 hours of consulting services
- Great Plains Software stepped forward with a free, first-year support plan in lieu of a lawsuit

From the implementation with Effective Company, we can observe a significant correction during the project that resulted in a final success. While this was a larger-than-average Dynamics GP implementation, the key components of the initial failure and the eventual effective management support are crystal clear and can be scaled down to any company.

Initially the key project stakeholders were uninvolved with services negotiation. In fact, no needs analysis, process flow, or project plan were prepared prior to the contract negotiations. The purchase of software, annual software plan, and services were reduced to simply a cost negotiation because the purchasing manager had no prior experience with business management system purchases. An accurate cost estimate for services, and sometimes even software components, can't be provided until a project plan is completed.

Before then, a service estimate is a dart thrown in pitch dark aiming at "industry standards."

The experienced new controller and IT manager had prepared a basic needs analysis and process workflow. My proposal built on those documents and was based upon a Gantt chart that mapped out the various tasks for data conversion, document design, prototyping, training, and implementation consulting. While this implementation involved more than the average number of Dynamics GP users, the design was straightforward.

No matter how well I plan, I always build in a contingency. I never know what any stakeholder might miss; I just know that there will always be a surprise feature or issue. In some circumstances, the client can't afford a surprise. Those cases require a complete implementation prototype rather than a scaled-down prototype.

Another successful component of Effective Company's implementation was their well-defined communication process. In addition to the weekly project meeting, all stakeholders were apprised weekly of the project progress. The Gantt chart on the wall was marked up. The controller was so proud that they were able to bring their second attempt at implementation in on budget and on time, the chart remained on the wall for two years after the implementation until the first upgrade plan took its place.

Choosing to put their energy into the implementation rather than into a lawsuit was a good choice facilitated by the developer's position to never allow a client to sue them.

In my regularly-scheduled project meetings with client project managers, I strive to cover any current or foreseeable impact on the budget and schedule. If there is a potential change in scope, I always offer the following options before I forge ahead with unauthorized hours:

- Does the client want to accommodate the change with internal resources?
- Does the client want to re-align resources and priorities to stay inside of the budget and timeframe?

- Does the client want the consultants to step up their contribution of resources to meet a scope change, recognizing the cost increase?

Case Study: Recession Company

One of our implementations was started in mid-2008 and completed September 1st, as the world economy was diving into the recession. The CEO of Recession Company called a company-wide meeting to kick off their project. He announced that the project was considered a business-critical change; although some employees might experience difficulty with the change, it was important for the company overall.

Further, he assigned 100 percent of the time of his new controller as project manager. The former controller would defer her retirement until the implementation was complete. He directed the new controller, "Do whatever it takes to make this implementation a success. You have complete authority to make any decisions needed."

The implementation was completed on time and under budget, as long as "under budget" accommodates two additional signed work authorizations:

1. The new controller determined the company's existing hardware wasn't able to handle the new software system so he purchased an additional server for roughly seven-thousand dollars.
2. He also indicated he wasn't familiar enough with the company to confidently document workflow processes and existing documentation didn't exist. He successfully persuaded the CEO to sign a seventeen-thousand dollars work authorization for our team to assess and document the current workflow processes for the four company locations.

During the two-month rapid implementation, the CEO was distracted with other issues. I neither saw nor spoke with him again until the project was completed.

Two weeks after the project was completed successfully, the CEO angrily communicated to me that the project was over budget; when he found out I had already been paid via lease financing, he was prepared to sue for the difference.

Some failures with Recession Company are obvious while others are more subtle. The chain of communication was broken in this company, and the directives by the CEO were inconsistent. It became apparent that he was distracted during the implementation.

Although he signed off on the purchase of the server and the additional work, when the project was completed, he didn't remember that there were additional authorized costs. Or didn't want to remember as this implementation started in July 2008 at the beginning of one of the worst financial recessions the world has ever seen.

Management support doesn't just mean, "Rah! Rah! Rah!" at the beginning of the project. That's clearly needed especially when the executive must state something to the effect of, "You, an individual, may not experience the benefit of this change, but I'm asking you for your support of the project for the good of the company overall." The executive at the kickoff meeting clearly sets the tone for project support.

Several aspects of this project demonstrate the impact of inconsistent messaging from executive management. The controller was new; he was uncomfortable with the needs analysis and process workflow documentation. He recognized the deficiency and asked for our assistance. The executive signed off on the change order.

That the server was deficient was obvious in the initial days of the implementation as the current one kept crashing. The executive signed off on this second change order. Once I finished the prototype, revised the Gantt chart and the project cost worksheet which then included the two changes, and assisted the client with financing that covered the entire project, the CEO also signed off on the financing documents containing a big, bold, underscored total of the project along with a statement directing the financing company to pay us the entire amount.

As a consultant, I've since refused to increase our services unless I experience **consistently** reasonable behavior. If the changes are truly agreed upon, signing the change order is easy. If there's a question or any hesitation, lack of a signature is good indication there's a problem. When the signatures have been obtained and yet the accusations fly, I withdraw from the implementation as quickly as I ethically can.

Aside from the unhappy ending, communication confusion, and budget accusations, the implementation was a success and did not progress into a lawsuit.

Case Study: Services Company

An implementation for a services company was kicked off in August several years ago. I agreed to a 100 hour project plan over two months. I agreed to provide project management and technical services. The client would complete online training webinars, data clean up, and system design with our review.

Ten months later the project was still incomplete. The services company restarted the project twice. The controller failed to keep deadlines and appointments. The owner kept delegating additional projects to his general manager; the manager had no choice but to engage his controller on most of those projects.

The owner stuck to his initial authorization of 100 hours, but we had little contact with him. To us, it simply appeared there was no executive oversight. The owner had a desire to upgrade his business management system, but he completely failed with providing resources to his manager.

As an owner, it isn't effective to purchase new software, dictate that your personnel implement it, but not make changes to how they work during the implementation. When I engage with a client that wants to be a DIY (Do-It-Yourself) implementation, I have a straightforward discussion about reallocation of personnel resources; I lose and they lose when they won't keep their promise.

I call an implementation with under allocation of resources for the duration a "broomstick" implementation. The client treats their consultant like a broom in the closet—an inanimate object with no needs of its own. They take me out only when they need me and perceive I should always be available and have no other projects or clients.

The problem being, I'm a very expensive resource. For survival in my industry, consultants must be billable at least seventy percent of their time. When a client consistently fails to meet deadlines and cancels my appointments, I have no choice but to push their project into my backlog queue. Even though I review the problems they're causing themselves and what the likely consequences will be as clearly as I can, frequently they don't recognize that it's a problem they control. I make a commitment to the next client, hopefully more consistent, and the broomstick implementation is in further jeopardy.

At that point the success of the implementation is out of my control; in my experience, most projects either fail or are severely compromised when they become a broomstick client.

Summary

Dedicating personnel to your project is the most important management support you can provide for your project. Effective management support means recognizing that an implementation project isn't something to squeeze in between "real work." If you can't afford professional consulting fees, use the best help that you can afford and dedicate them to the project.

The following are the ideas we provide to our clients to provide them with down-to-earth changes they can make to ensure a successful implementation. Some of these suggestions may seem beneath the executive to implement, but the more the executive understands about what the personnel are about to undertake, the more supportive he will be.

Choose the tips that are most effective for you, your implementation stakeholders, and your company. Consider using some of the tips some of the time; drop or add tips as relevant to your unique situation.

Tip	Comment on the Tip
Create a temporary workforce and project team.	Consider the use of temps, interns, and summer help. Your cost for this temporary work force is lower because you can avoid paying benefits. Bring back retired workers who are frequently glad to help for a period of time at lower rates. Former employees may be happy to have four hours a day of work during school hours or in between their college classes.
Hold a blue sky session with groups of workers.	Meet with no more than six at a time, all in a similar work group. Brainstorm how they can shift their work loads and defer tasks. Help your personnel shift their more routine work to the temporary work force. Don't bring the temporary work force in to learn the new system. Your regular employees must learn the new system.
Avoid yearend closing, audits, seasonal busy periods, and key staff vacations.	With powerful integration tools, we implement any time of the year or day of the month.
Don't expect your staff to put in excessive overtime.	In my thirty five years of experience, it's the rare person that can increase their work by five or ten hours a week for more than two weeks. They burn out, make major mistakes, and frequently quit right after you've paid for expensive training.
SMBs of less than twenty employees shouldn't implement when a key employee has a drop dead date of some kind.	Carefully consider the impact of events such as marriage and a two week honeymoon, a sabbatical, the once-in-a-lifetime vacation to Greece, and especially parental leave. I can guarantee the baby will be early or the implementation late—no exceptions to that in thirty five years. This isn't an endorsement to discriminate. Recognize the impact and accommodate for it by recognizing that training and expertise will be lost because the methodology isn't ingrained enough to stick after weeks or months of time off.

Implement in stages, not a Big Bang.	It's called a Sprint Cycle in project management terms. Systems have natural integration points where we're able to do a temporary integration of old and new systems. Phase the new system in. Between each phase, take a break of one to four weeks to allow your staff to catch up on their workload.
Don't run parallel.	Parallel runs triple the work load for your people. They operate the old system, operate the new system, and reconcile between the two systems. This is different than Sprint Cycles. If you choose to sprint, start with payables or receivables. Use the professional consultant to assist you with keeping your subsidiary ledgers in balance with their control accounts—posting integration must be tightly controlled.
Remove access to the old system except for key employees.	If the old system is still available, no one moves forward. I've seen failures where the employees revert to the comfortable old system, and we're called in for a second implementation (and a third, and, in one case, a fourth time).
Identify and deal with the holdouts before the implementation starts.	The holdouts can be such a major complication they're covered in Chapter IX.
Schedule your training sessions carefully in advance.	This tip affects your initial budgeting. It may take four hours to train customer service personnel, but you won't train all twelve of them at the same time. This issue alone can be the cause of your implementation services costing double or triple the initial estimate.
Prototype your system no matter how small your company and how simple your implementation.	If you must limit your investment in time and services, eliminate the needs analysis before eliminating the prototype.

Support the laughter and humor during training and implementation.	It's not a waste of time. Laughter helps employees retain information better.
Don't expect a new employee who used Dynamics GP five years earlier to go without training or be able to implement faster.	They're in the awkward situation of having to unlearn old functions and relearn new functions. In five years, the software has upgraded through two to three versions. An employee whose experience is more than a year old or a version old will require the same training as someone with no experience. I've seen this situation many times during my career. The employee simply doesn't have an accurate recall of the system. They make mistakes, frequently setup mistakes that are pervasive through the operation of the system. We don't regard a consultant as skilled enough to implement on their own until they've participated in six implementations.
Join a user group	Continue learning and teaching tips and tricks.
Set a time rule when obtaining support.	When I hire new consultants I give them a fifteen-minute rule: Struggle fifteen minutes to find the answer then ask for help. They learn multiple other things if not exactly what they're looking for, but they don't burn four hours looking for an answer I could give them in two minutes.
Develop a pyramid of help for your personnel.	First, fifteen minutes on their own, then they should go to their workgroup champion. If the workgroup champion can't resolve the issue, they both go to the company guru. Finally, everyone participates in a support call to your VAR. It helps to develop competency in your champions and guru.
Keep your annual plan current	You have access to free online help communities, training webinars, and thousands of technical help articles.
Don't defer setting up security in your system.	Thirty minutes is a whole lot cheaper on security set up than three days re-entering data accidentally deleted.

Meet regularly with your project team to review their progress.	Fridays or Mondays are good meeting days. Cover what was completed and applaud the progress. Plan what's going to be completed. If your project starts to fall behind, take action immediately. Adding resources to a project one week behind is easy. Finding out in three months it's off schedule is hopeless.
Facilitate effective project management	See Chapter IV for details.

II. Rapid Selection of Software

What you'll learn in this chapter:
- *Fifteen steps for rapid selection*
- *Rough estimates*
- *Strategic requirements that are much more important than functional requirements*

I won't cite a statistic for failure of business management system implementation failures because there are too many of them; it's simply a matter of what projects were studied by the consulting firm issuing the statistics. It doesn't matter who issued a statistic because it's always high. Double-digit high. When it's a big project failure, it's in the news. Many small projects fail though and those are the ones I'm writing about.

Business management system implementations start with selection of the software. In an effort to increase the number of implementation successes, I'll start with recommendations about the selection of software—tips and tricks to make the selection process more successful.

In my experience with many SMB prospects, the selection process is quick, implying that many steps of a typical selection process are skipped or abbreviated:

- It starts with the referral of the consultant from a trusted source
- A high level of trust is placed in the consultant and their company
- The demonstration isn't scripted—it's responsive to the prospect company's industry standards

The rapid implementation includes a nonexistent or abbreviated needs analysis and process workflow design. The prototype is merged with the needs analysis and enables an on-the-fly process workflow design. The project implementation style is both rapid and agile with the decisions, design, and implementation process flexing as discovery is made in the prototype.

Many SMBs can utilize a rapid implementation style in this manner with little in professional services as long as they begin with just financial modules—general ledger, payables, receivables, and bank reconciliation. As they advance into distribution modules—inventory, sales and purchase order processing—decisions get tougher and functionality becomes more critical.

If you do start with a simple financial module implementation on your own, choose a product with depth of functionality, third-party products, and consulting organizations, so once you complete implementation of the easy financial modules, you have the capability to keep building a system that can grow with your company.

If your company ultimately needs more than basic financial modules, strategic selection of the right software and consultant are vital. Manufacturing, project accounting, field service, and payroll modules, for example, require closer evaluation—the prototype is an excellent platform for this type of analysis.

If your rapid implementation also includes a rapid selection, I've updated a document of mine originally written over fifteen years ago. This time the document is oriented towards a rapid selection process, but still includes the steps for the functional requirements analysis and documentation.

Step 1–Form a Selection Committee

Form a selection committee limited in size so you can accomplish the project within a reasonable time period. This would be a common selection committee:

- CEO/President
- CFO/Controller/Accounting Manager
- IT Manager (not necessarily a fulltime employee in an SMB)
- Sales Manager
- Inventory Manager
- Purchasing Manager

It's important to have the CEO to provide strong executive steering, oversight, and management support. In my experience, half of system implementation failures are a result of the CEO not providing effective management support. See Chapter I for detailed actions you can take to provide effective management support.

Through the use of subcommittees and department meetings, gain input from the remainder of the company. It's important for every potential user of the system, including those who only receive reports from the system, to have input. Gaining all the input insures that you identify all necessary functionality. You also gain positive support with the participation of all employees.

Here's a good example of the members of the accounting subcommittee

- Payables lead person
- Receivables lead person
- Payroll lead person
- General Ledger lead person
- Collections manager

A common mistake is to include only accounting staff on the committees. Ultimately, the design of the system starts with the information reported. Think of your accounting staff as the people who input the information; everyone else is their customer receiving the product—the information from the system. The company can't ignore their customers, and the accounting staff shouldn't ignore their customers so include your customer service, sales, and warehouse staff.

Step 2–Select the Project Manager

Of the committee members, select a project manager. Free the project manager of their typical work load during the selection process. This is called "backfilling." Utilizing an employee already working full time, appointing them project manager without shifting their workload, is a common mistake. An implementation doubles their work load. From my experience, project managers that have not had their workload adjusted and been backfilled will burn out in an average of two weeks. That means they're useless for the rest of the project.

Utilize another employee or hire a temp to take on the routine tasks of the project manager during the implementation. Don't have a temp implement the new system.

If you appoint a project manager who has never managed a major project and fail to provide them with training and tools, plus don't relieve them of their other workload, you are certainly headed for trouble.

Step 3–Develop Primary Strategic Goals

Strategic goals center on what you are trying to achieve and how you are going enhance your company's profitability, productivity, and ability to compete. Here are good sample strategic goals, but this is a key area for your company to uniquely define.

Goals: Implement an integrated accounting and web accessible system:

- Capable of facilitating the company's growth over the next decade,
- That reduces and eliminates double entry of data into nonintegrated systems,
- That provides accurate and timely financial and management reports,
- That allows us to better track inventory and helps us to reduce our inventory on hand, and
- That allows us to convert quotes into orders, and orders into invoices, so we can facilitate our sales process and be more professional with our customers.

Step 4–Identify the Infrastructure

Deployment Onsite

Identify the components of your system, selecting a central platform. This will help you identify from which software products you should select. The market has shaken out in the last decade to four probable central platforms for business systems:

- The dominant midmarket share is held by Microsoft server and Microsoft SQL database
- Novell server and LINUX database hold a modest midmarket share
- Various servers with an Oracle database in the tier one market, the high end
- Application centric databases unique to entry level products and miscellaneous niche products in the midmarket

It's expensive to purchase software products across two or more central platforms. It takes a different technical department or contractor to support each central platform. If you have two central platforms, you've just doubled your IT costs. Only large companies would utilize both Microsoft SQL and LINUX, for example.

Hosted Deployment

The Internet has made business management possible without any central platform. Whatever desktop, laptop, or notebook computer you have, if it can access the Internet, you may utilize hosted software deployed through an Internet browser. If this is the way you decide to go, see Chapter VI.

Step 5–Determine the Estimated Budget

My experience is that SMBs spend from one half percent to four percent of their gross annual revenue implementing a business management system. An onsite deployment has significantly different costs than a hosted deployment. Both deployments show ranges of functionality and modules; both can have substantially wide variance due to many factors, including:

- Technical inclination of the company
- Level of a mature deployment with advanced modules
- Degree of obsolescence of the legacy system
- Accuracy of legacy data
- Desired amount of legacy data imported
- Participation of internal staff in contrast to professional services
- Number of modules implemented
- Number of users
- Type of training

Onsite

	Low	High
Server, operating system, peripheral equipment	$12,000	$16,000
Dynamics GP 2013 for 8 users	$20,000	$40,000
First year software maintenance plan	$6,000	$10,000
Estimated professional services	$30,000	$60,000
Estimated total first year cost	$68,000	$126,000

Hosted

	Low	High
Monthly cost for 8 users	$1,380	$1,800
Estimated professional services	$30,000	$60,000
Estimated total first year cost	$46,560	$81,600

Regardless of the cost to deploy, many other factors come into play to compute the return on investment. We once deployed fifty companies, migrating the data from their parent company's enterprise software to Dynamics GP. The enterprise software licenses they would have purchased would have cost two million dollars. The Dynamics GP implementation, while costing $250,000, was less than they would have paid for annual maintenance of the other software.

To validate your investment, begin with the recovery period you desire: one year, three years, five years, or whatever is appropriate in your case. Compute the value of the benefits you expect to receive against your cost estimates. Your system should pay for itself within your selected recovery period in areas like these:

- Is your current system limiting your company's growth? How much profit gain you recognize with a new system?
- What does it cost to do the double and triple entry of information common with nonintegrated systems?
- Identify what mistakes are costing you and how much you'll gain by reducing or eliminating those mistakes
- Will your bank charge you a lower rate of interest on your line of credit if you provide them with better information?
- Determine the cost of carrying excess inventory by determining how much you'll gain in cash flow if you reduce inventory by ten or fifteen percent.
- Determine how much inventory you've lost through "shrinkage" (theft), spoilage, obsolescence, and waste.
- Compute the annual cost of extra employees to handle the work of the sales order process.

Step 6–Develop a Timeframe

The rapid implementation can take two days up to four months. For the midmarket company, a standard implementation can take two to four months. It's all a matter of relativity. The idea is: create an estimated timeline that meets your needs.

Your estimate for implementation time may change after your prototype. Implement at your slack time of the year. Setup a sinking fund during your busy season so you have the funds to implement during the slack season. Implement before your company's growth spurt.

Yearend Implementations

In general, your accounting staff is already too busy at yearend to ask them to be involved in an implementation project. Industry standard midmarket software has the integration tools to import historical data so you can implement at any time of the year. Even payroll can be implemented mid-year, mid-quarter, or mid-month.

Step 7–Develop Functional Requirements

Developing a list of detailed functional requirements is usually a difficult task for staff in SMB companies. Sound processes may not be in place with either manual processes or legacy computer systems, yet personnel look for new software to do things in a familiar way. Strive to strike a balance between recognizing when the software must change to suit your business versus when the software's predefined processes would be better.

A successful procedure to follow is to develop a questionnaire to distribute throughout your company. Encourage personnel to look at their key processes, reports, and information, and answer these types of questions:

- How does information come to me?
- How do I process and report information?
- What is most important about that information?
- What works well about how I handle that information?
- What could be done better, faster, and easier?

The information that you gather should facilitate discussions by the project team and subcommittees, eventually resulting in the preparation of a written Functional Requirements Definition. Here are samples:

General requirements:

- Consistent, easy-to-use interface
- Security restrictions on forms
- Drilldown capability
- Easy to import and export data
- Flexible data fields

Financial requirements:

- Flexible general ledger account code
- Multicurrency capability
- Recurring and reversing journal entry types
- Batch and immediate posting methods
- Bank reconciliation

Sales requirements

- Commission calculation and reporting
- Sales tax calculation and reporting
- Quote, order, invoice, and return documents

Purchasing requirements

- Purchase requisitions
- Purchase orders
- Purchase returns
- Purchasing receipts automatically generate vouchers

Inventory

- Serial or lot number control
- Multiple costing methodologies
- Complex pricing methodologies
- Multiple location and bin management

Payroll

- Unless preparing payroll is a competitive advantage, outsource payroll to a service

Step 8–Request Information

Make a few phone calls to start contact with the software vendor—the developer directly, resellers in your area, or an individual consultant. Be prepared to provide them with a simple RFI (Request for Information). Too much at this point is a waste of your time and theirs. Lack of anything written means you'll be stating it over and over and over and also indicates your lack of preparation, organization, and management support.

Different reseller organizations have different policies about a RFI. Some round file every one sent to them believing that the relationship is so key, if they had no advance warning that an RFI was coming, they're simply being used as "column fodder"—you have no intention of buying from them; you simply needed three quotes.

Invest a little time in making the initial contact and building a positive strategic relationship if you want multiple quality responses.

Provide this Written Information

- Your company background – what your company does, how many employees you have, note if you extensively use subcontractors
- Summary financial information on gross revenue and anticipated growth rate
- Your budget and timeframe estimate
- A short statement on your preferred deployment method and whether you're open to options
- Stipulation of how and when they should contact your selection committee leader
- Provide your strategic criteria

Request this Written or Electronic Information

- Their corporate, employee, and solution profiles and contact information.
- Brief description of their training policies and procedures
- Customer testimonial sheets or references in your industry, stressing that you will not call references until you are explicitly granted authorization to do so
- Information on recommended hardware, operating system, and database requirements for your software
- Software fact sheets describing:
  - The underlying database
  - All available modules of the software
  - Reporting and development tools usable with the software

Don't Request a Software Demonstration Yet

Demonstrations are typically requested prematurely because companies are seeking software that's easy to use. The problem that I see frequently, the easiest to use software doesn't have the required depth of functionality, and the software developer or reseller aren't viable for the long term. Seek a business partner and a software product at this stage of your selection process that ensures you of a strong foundation for your business management system.

Seek a Financially Stable Software Developer Capable of Keeping Pace with Technology

Software developers know their survival rests on their business foundation, strong financial strength, and strong insight into the market, mainstream databases, and development tools. Successful, stable financial management packages are owned by a handful of developers who have withstood the test of twenty or more years. We encourage you to select software from those vendors. Seek a product roadmap from that vendor that indicates you have at least a ten-year path with the product under evaluation and its successor.

Seek a Software Developer with a Redundant Base of Local VARs (Value Added Resellers)

These are the independent companies, usually locally owned and operated, who sell the software and will be your primary "go to" for training, implementation services, and support. Your reseller should have a demonstrated track record of providing after sale support. The software developers will have multiple VARs in major metropolitan centers.

The average VAR has eight employees although this number is increasing due to software developer pressures. Determine if they have customers who've worked with them more than two years. Rely on redundancy because VAR's go in and out of business frequently; mergers are common, and competitive pressures are causing them to increase in size.

Determine if the lead installer has completed at least six installations of the current version of software. Get to know this person well. Like any other good professional, you will likely follow them wherever they work. Having multiple VARs and installers to choose from provides you with alternatives and backup.

Seek a Product Available on Your Preferred Deployment Model and Central Platform

I frequently encounter SMBs that have multiple central platforms because their personnel drive the selection based purely on user interface or functionality. The IT department is then driven to support multiple central platforms. This fact alone drives up the cost of the software.

Then integration of data between the systems and platforms becomes a major issue causing inaccuracy, instability, and further expense. Integration of data between systems and the cost of technical support should drive you to select only one central platform.

It is possible, although extremely rare, that software providing your unique competitive advantage may exist on only one type of central platform. If that's the case, selection of the central platform and the software for your competitive advantage must occur first. Then follow with financial software or whatever business management software is also available on that central platform.

Seek Software Capable of Growing With Your Company

The key underlying industry standard database capabilities facilitate growth with scalability. The database is what provides for integration, reporting, and customization. The software may have a low entry point with additional modules or groups of modules that can be added for additional cost. Then there will be a following of third-party modules.

Over the last decade in the midmarket, Microsoft and Sage have demonstrated scalability with their various products. Microsoft is unique with both technical tools for upgrading through their four ERP (Enterprise Resource Planning) systems in addition to allowing for transfer of license investment.

Sage owns multiple software systems, but their strategy is focused more on purchase and hold rather than upgrade and transferability. As this book was going to market, Sage announced the sunset of their MAS 500 product in five years.

NetSuite is a rising star with their pure SaaS model. Companies can start with NetSuite then add One World.

Seek Software Accompanied by Industry standard Development Tools

Using the Microsoft central platform as an example, the software systems that you evaluate should be capable of linking to Access, Excel, Word, Visual Basic, Visual Studio, and SQL Server Reporting Services—all Microsoft tools. In addition, well known products like Crystal Reports should link to the software system.

Seek a Product with a Large Following of Third party Developers

Third party developers satisfy the needs of vertical and niche markets. The third party developer builds their products around popular midmarket software. It's in their best interest to have access to the largest market share so they associate with the most popular, stable, established midmarket software with easy, functional, and flexible integration capability.

Capitalize on the research third party developers have already completed. Choose business management software with a large following of third party developers. With continuity going back to the 1980's and 1990's Microsoft ERP software has thousands of third party developers.

The Sage 100 and 500 products have thousands of third party developers, but Sage recently announced its plan to sunset the MAS 500 product.

NetSuite launched its marketplace to attract ISVs in 2009 hoping for ten participants. It's acquired hundreds since then.

Oracle announced its cloud based product, Fusion, in October 2012.

Seek an Established Reseller

Take the time to make a short visit to your resellers' offices. Many installation specialists work out of home offices, small professional offices, or executive office suites. The small operators will tell you that they're working on client site frequently so there's no need for an expensive office. That may have been true in 2008 to 2010 when everyone was cutting expenses in order to survive, but now they should be back in offices with support and administrative staff.

Some reseller organizations are large with multiple satellite personnel. That's perfectly acceptable, but if you're working with one of those satellite consultants, develop an understanding of the reseller's support system and how their headquarters operates. When I first started in this business, it was acceptable to use the home office desk and a brick-sized cell phone. Not anymore.

Seek a Product with Alternative Methods for Training and Support

Support alternatives should be abundant. You should have the choice of calling your consultant directly when an issue is unique to a current, active project although a support desk at the headquarters is invaluable. An online technical database open to search 24/7 is fundamental.

The software developer should provide several alternatives for pay on demand support, packs of support incidents, and prepaid unlimited support plans with several levels of guaranteed response time.

Classroom training, webinars, manuals, custom classes, and brush up training resources should be available.

Seek Business Partners with Industry Experience

Your level of comfort with your software developer, reseller, and installation consultant will increase dramatically as they provide references from other companies like yours. I have encountered situations where clients appreciate my industry experience and other situations when clients are concerned about the potential leak of confidential information. I recommend going with the industry experience and a well-written confidentiality agreement.

Step 9–Evaluate the Responses and Schedule Meetings

Now's the time when you should shorten your list of products, resellers, and consultants. If they're slow responding, maybe they're the industry specialist worth waiting for or maybe they're just not organized. Maybe they're overwhelmed and won't be able to assist you with a rapid implementation.

I assisted an Arizona not for profit association with an RFI several years back. We sent out over a dozen RFI's, cut our list down to six products, and got to the point where a committee member was assigned to each one for the initial demonstration. One of our leading contenders then stopped responding. We sadly got to a point where we eliminated them from the process then found out they had just declared bankruptcy. Response to initial contact is as telling as performance during the prototype and live implementation.

Step 10–Meet with the Selected Resellers

Meet with the selected software resellers. Be prepared for a mutual question and answer session. If you're not comfortable with any reseller but like the software, call the software developer and insist they put another reseller in touch with you. After this step is completed you should have no more than three resellers and three software packages ranked according to your preferences.

Step 11–Request a Demonstration

Now the rapid selection starts to differ from the standard selection process. If you making a rapid selection, view a generic—although industry-specific—demonstration. If you're taking more time with less risk, request a scripted demonstration.

A Rapid, Industry-specific Demonstration

This demonstration may be completely online and generic if you're looking for very straightforward financial functionality. If you're working with a reseller and consultant, their industry-specific demonstration will typically last two to four hours. It may be provided at your site or remotely.

If you're making a rapid selection and it's critical to keep your costs down, you must insure you have the willingness to change your processes to fit the software. With too many prospects I hear, "Sure, we'll change our processes to industry standards." Then the complaints start about what the new software won't do unique to them.

Insure that your selection committee is prepared to attend the demonstrations relating to their areas of interest. I consider the attendance at demonstrations an indicator of the success of the implementation. If you as an owner or manager can't get your team to the demonstration, you likely won't be effective in supporting an implementation.

Members of the selection committee should take notes during each demonstration to accurately and completely track the presentations and feedback. If they watch two or more demonstrations and don't take notes, they'll confuse products.

The selection committee should cycle through their questions and the reseller's responses until they've isolated a single reseller and software as their preferred choice. Advise the other resellers of your choice, but also let them know you might return to their product. Be prepared for some sales pressure at this point. Read Chapter VIII on choosing the right reseller to understand the situation. Or "go dark" and just refuse to communicate with the other resellers. We're pretty wise when someone takes that tactic. Just don't lead them on.

A Company and Data-specific Scripted Demonstration

If you need complex functionality, you'll need to prepare a detailed functional requirements definition to your selected resellers providing two to four weeks of preparation time for them.

Step 12–Check Customer References

Once you've selected your preferred vendor and software, I recommend calling customer references rather than making site visits. Site visits show you how other companies use software, not how the software will work for you. Don't expect another company to show you how they process transactions or produce financial statements. Their data is usually confidential.

Here are some good questions to ask references, although pick just the ones most important to you:

- How many software solutions did you consider and why?
- What were your strategic requirements?
- Why did you select your software? You may become aware of reasoning that heavily swayed their decision that's not relevant for your company.
- What modules are you using? If this company is similar to you and you find they're not using a module you're contemplating, drill down more on this information. Maybe you'll find out they consider it unnecessary, cumbersome, or overly complex.
- From whom did you originally purchase the software and are they still supporting you? Their answer may tell you which resellers to avoid if they have switched.
- Who was the vendor's lead consultant for your project?
- Who were the other consultants on your project? Tell me about the quality of their work.
- What style of training did you use?
- Did you have data conversion and integration during start up? This is often a difficult step. The more information you have, the better.
- Describe to me your "Go Live" date/time.
- Who do you call when you need critical support?
- Who do you call when you need routine support?
- Do you have any customizations to the software? Explore this issue if it's relevant to you.

- Do you have custom reports? Explore this issue if it's relevant to you.
- How often do you upgrade?
- What happens during a typical upgrade?
- What do you like most about the software?
- What do you like least about the software?
- What do you like least about your reseller/consultant?
- What do you like most about your reseller/consultant?
- What are your plans with your business solution over the next few years?
- What would you do differently about the purchase of your software?
- What would you do differently about the implementation of your software?
- Do you have any recommendations for us?

Step 13–Prepare a Prototype

At this point you've screened software developers, software, resellers, and consultants for your strategic criteria, budget, and timeframe. You've observed at least one thorough demonstration of the software and screened the reseller's customer references. You're confident you've chosen a good business solution and reseller.

You're ready to prototype. See Chapter XII for the details.

Step 14–Refresh the Implementation Plan

The prototype was the litmus test. In my opinion, many business management system implementation projects are considered failed or compromised because the plan was wrong, not the project. Businesses want to lock down the budget and timeframe before they've done adequate planning to forecast a reasonable implementation plan, cost, and timeframe.

See Chapter VIII about picking the right vendor and understanding your vendor's situation. If you've lowered your risk by deferring costs as much as possible (see the Chapter XII on ways the Prototype can help you defer costs), you'll be in a much stronger position to assess the real cost and timeframe for your implementation.

Step 15–Engage and Implement

At this point you should have:

- The right software
- A reliable software developer, reseller, and consultant
- An accurate picture of costs and timeframe

Case Study: Summary

I was recently contacted by a former client—a CFO who specialized in SMB financial and operational turnarounds. I first met him when he assisted a retiring SMB owner with the sale of his company.

The CFO was again turning around an SMB in which he had purchased equity. He contacted me when he realized the business management system needed to be upgraded. One of the first things I did was provide him with a draft of this chapter. His response to me was, "You really dropped a bomb on me."

I gasped because he made his statement to me while I was with all of his key employees in our first meeting. He instantly saw my horror and reassured me by saying, "It was a good bomb. You made me realize we weren't ready."

So they're taking a few weeks to get ready based on a few more draft chapters—my first win and I haven't gone to press yet.

III. Get Your Ducks in a Row

What you'll learn in this chapter
- *Key characteristics for a successful rapid implementation*
- *How to recognize when personnel don't have adequate resources*
- *How to recognize when you aren't using the right personnel for a project*
- *Other company issues that may impact a rapid implementation*

Key Characteristics of a Company's Potential for a Successful Rapid Implementation

You don't start out wishing to exceed your budget, blow past your planned schedule, and fail to obtain the functionality you need. All implementations have primary goals of being on time, on budget, and meeting functionality requirements.

While there are many reasons for project success, in this chapter we'll address the key ones. If you do the following three things well, you'll substantially increase your potential for a successful project.

1. The project manager was exclusively committed and key personnel had a substantial amount of their time committed to the project
2. Personnel committed to the project were screened for behaviors known to facilitate project success
3. The project was flexible with the Go Live date within reason; in order to be clear, I recommend up to a month of flexibility.

Good people committed to their project can successfully complete the project. From the onset of the project, you should be asking yourself these questions:

- Are you meeting key milestones?
- Are personnel behaving like they are committed to the project?
- Are you effectively setting aside or reassigning other priorities?

Implementations completed on time are usually successful. It's usually an indication they were well planned and provided with adequate resources. However, you can't wait for the Go Live date to determine if you're going to be successful. Depending on the timeframe for your project, you need to start measuring yourself the first week. In a two-week implementation, start measuring yourself the first day and keep measuring daily. Kick off your week or your day with a plan of what's going to happen next.

Late implementations are usually failures. Timing is usually the first thing that slips. Throw up the penalty flag and start looking for the problem as soon as your project falls behind. Just as "life happens," work happens. The stresses and demands on the project team from their other work will build up and further erode your schedule as soon as you open a crack.

Implementations with dedicated personnel are usually successful. Most people like to work—it's an instinct with adults to be productive. Good people who enjoy their work do good work. Unless you're dealing with passive aggressive behavior or personnel with overwhelming personal problems, your project team is going to want to get the project work done when they have no other distractions or priorities. The job of the project manager is to keep the implementation work in front of the team to make it the easiest choice of which work to complete. Just as people like to work, they enjoy the work that they're comfortable with and in which they're knowledgeable.

Implementations are usually failures when there isn't a strong project manager and when personnel haven't received management support to reallocate their work load.

Common Personnel Behaviors in a Failing Project

We see these behaviors in so many implementation projects, they are early warning signs of personnel that aren't on target:

- Cancelled appointments at the last minute to take care of day-to-day work emergencies. I've tracked implementations where this problem alone increases the project service cost by as much as twenty percent.
- Late start appointments because personnel must take care of emergencies for which no one else is prepared to deal with
- Lack of concentration in training classes because of emails, phone calls, and interruptions. The class time is drawn out with more expensive consulting hours and retention of the material is poor. The implementation moves more slowly than projected.
- Failure to clean and transform data for import, causing the consultant to defer integration or perform out-of-scope data cleaning.

Are Your Personnel the Right Personnel for the Project?

By now you'll have picked up on the issue that a major component of management support means providing adequate staffing for your implementation and providing that they have adequate time to devote to the project. Beyond that, you must have a good feeling about whether they are the right personnel for the job.

It still makes me take pause and pale a little when an SMB owner tells me his people are smarter and work harder than people at other companies. I immediately know we're going to have a problem implementation. The reality is that SMBs don't have an advantage during an implementation project with smarter, harder working people.

SMBs simply have the need to get the project done with less time and fewer resources and expertise. Most SMBs have really good people, but people and implementation projects using new business management software are unique combinations every time, and business owners and managers don't always assess the combination accurately.

Just because your people are good at their jobs, you should question whether they're the right people for the project. Several years back I was talking with the president of a client—a client of mine since 1993 and one whose employee holiday party I've attended for over a decade. Bob's an engineer of very few words. I advised him I needed to take time to prepare a project plan to implement job costing. Relating it to his work so I thought he would better agree, I inserted my foot in my mouth by pointing out that he wouldn't start to build one of his products without an engineering diagram and parts list.

He laughed and told me, "Well, actually, we're so experienced with some of our designs, we just pace them out on the production floor." Experienced personnel may overcome many challenges during a project to achieve a successful outcome, but those projects and successful outcomes generally involve their competitive business operations.

Part of the problem is that the implementation process is substantially different than day-to-day operation of the system, and the required skill sets of the personnel are different. That isn't to say, have the consultant implement a system for you then turn it over to you. Accept that an implementation is a complex process requiring skills your employees may not have and don't need on a daily basis. Back in the 1990's we were training personnel crossing the chasm from DOS to Windows. The first training classes we held were Windows classes. We still replace fifteen year-old green-screen systems and read RFI's that request a mouse interface.

The jump from a typical entry level implementation to a well-done, on-budget business management system implementation can be staggering for an SMB. With an entry-level implementation, SMBs have frequently spent less than $5,000 on software and engaged little or no hours of professional implementation services. They were successful because there aren't a lot of decisions to be made with entry-level software.

However, the greater the cost of the software, the greater the complexity of the software; therefore, successful midsize implementations take a lot more resources. I recognize that the desire is to pull those out of the hat without shelling out the big bucks. Accurately assessing your personnel to insure they are the right ones to complete your project is one of the biggest challenges you'll face and one of the most vital to the project's success.

Qualities in an Internal Project Manager

If you haven't engaged a professional project manager, look for these qualities and attributes in your employees:

- In a small company, the project leader is likely to be the financial person—a CFO, controller, accounting manager, or bookkeeper.
- Alternatively, your IT manager may have project management experience.
- They should be well organized. If their office looks like a disaster zone, if only they can find a document, I'd recommend you rethink your choice.
- Their documentation and planning skills should be excellent. They won't be afraid of using Microsoft Excel or even Microsoft Project.
- Their communication skills are excellent. You shouldn't have heard of communication failures surrounding your project manager.
- They should participate in the software and consultant selection process. Much more on this topic in the chapters about selecting software and a vendor.
- They must be unequivocally enthusiastic about the project. This is a key determinant so there will be multiple examples of failures in this book so you know what common attributes to watch out for.
- The project manager should be adept with computers and software—comfortable with email, documentation, and spreadsheets.

Those are the positive attributes. Read Chapter V on project management, Chapter IX on the holdout, Chapter X on other assessments, and Chapter XI on prioritization.

If you find yourself hesitant to proceed with a project, if you see your project with too many of the problems covered in this book, I highly recommend you take the silver bullet approach. Contact your software developer, reseller, or consultant. Or contact the silver bullets cited on page x.

IV. A Firm's Rapid Implementation Success

In this chapter you'll learn:
- *What not to do for a rapid implementation*
- *How to have a successful outcome despite the problems*

Case Study: Architectural Firm

An early rapid implementation is still number one on my list of difficult implementations. It took a team effort just six weeks from ordering of the hardware and software to sending the first new customer statements out. Software and hardware cost half a million dollars plus the cost of a five-person department swollen to fourteen people for six months.

The rocky start to the implementation was brought on when the firm's administrator walked into the server room and pulled the old Wang minicomputer's power cord out of the power supply stating, "This damn thing doesn't work!" She was right, especially because she caused a hard crash of the disk drive from which the old Wang didn't recover.

Many of you sweet young things have never heard of a Wang minicomputer. Honest, they were a hot ticket twenty-eight years ago. Our disk drive was a whopping 684 megabytes—multiple platters stacked like records into an enclosure the size of a washing machine. Twenty eight years ago, software systems required time intensive compilation, configuration, set up, and re-indexing. Backups of the 684 megabytes of data ran all night.

After pulling the plug, armed with a blank check, the administrator hopped onto a plane for an East coast developer and ordered the delivery of the new hardware and software the next day.

Once she returned to Portland, the administrator knew she needed someone with implementation skills so she approached a competitive firm in town which she knew had an IT manager with experience in the software just purchased. She worked out an agreement for the IT manager, Shirley, to work eighty percent of the time for the Architectural Firm and twenty percent of her time for the other firm. In addition, the accounting team was expanded for six months from five to fourteen individuals. Eventually a fifteenth person was added.

Architectural Firm's controller was upset by the authority taken from her and granted to Shirley, so she walked off the job without notice. A new controller was hired during his first interview. Several days later he announced he was going out for coffee in the afternoon and never came back. He didn't answer his home phone, but did cash the final check mailed to him so no foul play was suspected in his disappearance.

A few days later I was interviewed and hired by a three-person computer committee and also started the same afternoon as my interview. Fortunately and unfortunately, I stayed on the job after finding out the history.

I had multiple meetings with the software developer's technical consultant and Shirley. After the first few days of getting my feet on the ground, I had a private meeting with Shirley. She and I weren't confident of the consultant's commitment to going live within thirty days, and Shirley was clearly overwhelmed getting the hardware and software simply operative in time. Plus we were all concerned about the late delivery of two optical character readers, the OCR's.

Backed by the computer committee members and Shirley, I took the authority as project manager from the consultant and placed it upon myself. He was a little huffy, but he got over it once he saw the planning and scheduling that was about to take place.

Between the software consultant, Shirley, and I, we divided the implementation into three clear areas of responsibility. The software consultant trained and managed the five billing clerks. Shirley was totally engrossed in the hardware and software customization, compilation, and indexing. I managed my other nine staff people, reconciling the historical AR (Accounts Receivable) and

WIP (Work in progress) while managing the daily routines of an accounting staff supporting a professional services firm.

I moved my office furniture around to clear a ten by fifteen foot wall to create our first project plan with sticky notes. They wouldn't stick on the wood paneling so I sent a clerk down to the local five and dime store for red yarn and thumbtacks. Wrapping the red yarn around the tacks, I created several critical paths. Three critical paths converged on the OCR's arrival and successful operation. The project plan was innovative to the professionals in the firm and many of them came up to my office to see the wall.

I'm not much of a large committee decision person, but I sat through numerous meetings while the secretaries discussed how addresses should be formatted, how punctuation and abbreviations would be consistently utilized. The secretaries all used modern Selectric typewriters. New elements—font balls—were ordered for typing the timecards so the backordered OCR's wouldn't have to be reconfigured for different fonts. It continued to be obvious to the project team that the OCR's were the critical component of the entire project.

At about the four week mark, the OCR's arrived. The month's 20,000 timecards were ready. Shirley spent the night scanning and processing the bills for thirty secretaries and five new billing clerks to review the next day. We were right on schedule. Unbelievably, we made the deadline. No...we thought we made the deadline.

Then we determined that every time entry was in tenths of an hour, and every digit of "1" scanned as the letter "l" as in "long." You got it. Every time entry was wrong; 20,000 of them were wrong; and it would take a long time to correct all of them.

Architectural Firm had operated for decades with a policy of paying all bills at the end of the month, holding back enough cash to last about ten days, and dispersing the remainder of funds to the firm partners. It had no credit line. The bank would gladly extend a credit line, but that would require a bank audit of WIP and AR—records which were in complete disarray.

Today, a sharp SQL programmer could script a replacement of "el" with "1" in minutes. Today, time entry would be done directly into the system by the professional or their secretary; the time entry field wouldn't allow the input of a character. In 1984, it was beyond the skill set of the firm's professionals to have a computer on their desk. In 1984, it was beyond the capacity of the software and its developers to convert the character in the field.

Hourly personnel weren't allowed to work without a salaried manager on site so Shirley and I split twelve-hour shifts for eight days supervising our team while they edited every time entry. We had a five-user license because we planned for five billing clerks, so we had five stations going twenty four hours a day for eight days. I was banned from the server room by Shirley because my skirt had the uncanny habit of crashing the drives with static electricity with the slightest contact with the drive enclosure despite the elevated antistatic floor.

The administrator nurtured Shirley and I. Lunches were brought in; personal errands were run for us; my husband and daughters were invited in during the evenings for dinner at the office with mom. I had a cot set up in my office. That nugget of nurturing is included here with a grimace as I'll also add that, of course, this was my first job after vowing I would never do another implementation in my life.

This implementation was clearly in jeopardy several times. A number of concrete actions made it ultimately successful. The management team of the firm empowered the administrator and the computer committee members with decision-making authority. SMB teams are nimble. SMB teams burdened with responsibility for success under stress must be endowed with authority.

Shirley and I met with the computer committee briefly every day. When we had a crisis, the computer committee members had an open door policy. When we needed more resources, we had immediate access to the managing partners.

I provided weekly cash reports in lieu of financial reports for three months. We made critical decisions during implementation to leave historical data behind. It was junk anyway. The majority of the system was in the client billing system, so that's where we concentrated all of our efforts in the six-week implementation.

While there were many other technical and strategic decisions made to facilitate this rapid implementation, the key ones to focus on are those driven by executive management personnel. Management support wasn't a blank check and a directive to implement. It was active, frequent executive support, regular meetings, and reprioritization of routines like financial reporting.

The implementation team took pause to create a project plan. An agile project team was empowered with both responsibility and authority. We had a strategy and process that effectively dealt with surprise crises. I have never completed a project when there wasn't some sort of surprise. Sometimes the surprise is small; sometimes it's a showstopper. Management and personnel attitudes and flexibility make the surprise crisis a showstopper or merely a problem to resolve.

Summary of Effective Management Support and What was Right

- Financial support
- Change management facilitated
- Empowerment of an agile project team with authority
- Reprioritizing of routines for a period of time
- Increased number of staff
- Engagement of staff and consultants with implementation experience
- Selection of a software program uniquely designed for the firm's industry

Project Failures

- Advance planning was totally absent
- The only needs analysis was verbal
- There was no time for a prototype
- Effective staffing ultimately happened primarily by luck
- Project services were over budget.
- Detailed technical specifications weren't provided by the software developer.
- Project was over schedule

When the administrator initially pulled the Wang's plug, the problem had been caused by poorly designed, untested customization of the software, a much older version of the same software the firm was about to implement. Both WIP (work in process) and AR (accounts receivable) accounts were fragmented. WIP entries were typed in by the secretaries and the only view of a client account was via a billing report for the entire database. When the billing report was printed, the first account was partially printed on page 1, finished on page 50, and duplicated in its entirety on page 200. Obtaining an accurate amount of WIP and AR was impossible; both values were estimated at about $1,000,000 each.

The fifteenth employee, a temporary employee who loved to reconcile messes, took six months to eventually identify $5,000,000 in WIP and $3,000,000 in AR. I was treated like a mass murderer when I made that announcement at a partner meeting. With some of the WIP up to two years old, the collection effort would be huge. I don't know how much the firm eventually collected; I got out of Dodge and moved on to my next project—the birth of my youngest daughter.

V. KISS Project Management for Dragon Slayers

What you'll learn in this chapter
- *Tips and tricks with project management*
- *What is and isn't effective project management*

Project management is a career. You can find professional organizations, certified project managers, and countless books and articles about how to run a project to correctly select and implement a system. You'll find many dry but accurate books on:

- Implementation methodology
- Project management
- Lean implementation

The fairy god mother has blessed you if you get through these. This is my market and I struggle with those reads. These books emphasize planning, project management, process analysis, and management support. **_These books are right on the mark_**. But do SMBs follow this advice?

No. They simply don't have the time, money, expertise, or desire.

Happy endings in fairy tales are fun to believe, but the truth is that business management system implementations usually don't have happy endings unless the client purchases more implementation services than they thought they needed. I'll recite the reasons in Chapter VIII, but I'll also comment in that chapter on another reason which people in my industry don't like to talk about.

I can be this brutally honest, no citations needed here, because I've been a user, buyer, advisor, or consultant involved with software system implementations for thirty-five years.

Projects in Jeopardy

If you're reading this book because you have a failing project, I highly recommend you set this book and your project aside and take the time to read Todd C. Williams's book, *Rescue the Problem Project: A Complete Guide to Identifying, Preventing, and Recovering from Project Failure (AMACOM)*.

In addition, look for resources from Project Management Institute, www.pmi.org, which has been around for decades. There are other theories and certifications including Scrum Project Management (start at www.scrumdesk.com) and Microsoft's newer Sure Step methodology (most information retained only within secure Microsoft Partner websites) geared specifically to the Dynamics product line.

All of these project management theories and practices describe similar types of projects that include agile and rapid methodology. Your certified Microsoft reseller is required to have at least two consultants on staff certified in Sure Step project management. If you can afford any services, obtain the project manager's services, but interview your project manager as closely as you would interview a new employee.

Case Study: Quasi-state Agency

I began engagement in a large project in 2006 as the lead Dynamics GP technical consultant. The client hired another person as the project manager; someone with other business management system implementation experience, but she was unfamiliar with Dynamics GP. There were other problems with this project that you can read about in the Chapter XXVII on culture wars, but the project management was the last deciding factor for me to disengage immediately after the kickoff meeting.

Over 100 people were involved with the project so the kickoff meeting was split into two sessions. The two meetings overlapped long enough to engage in a team-bonding activity. We were divided into groups of five to seven people, given crayons, and a choice of animal pictures taken from a child's coloring book. The drawings were taped together to form a "totem pole" to depict the nature of each team. It was at that point I determined my head cold was a good excuse to leave the meeting.

The next day I bowed out of the project as gracefully as possible. What I saw that day convinced me this was failure waiting to happen. The first phase was simply the needs analysis and prototype, estimated as a $1,000,000 project by itself. The live implementation was estimated at $1,500,000. The needs analysis and prototype project went double over budget and time; the live implementation was never completed.

In my opinion, a professional project manager for a business management solution should:

- Be technically familiar with the product
- Hold a PMI, Scrum, or Sure Step project management certification
- Have implemented or managed at least six similar implementations—the same industry with the same product
- Use appropriate and relevant project management techniques, including team bonding events. You'll know it when you see it. You are the best judge of what are appropriate and relevant activities and techniques for your company. If you're the owner or general manager, you set the tone.
- Be flexible to modify methodology for the situation, especially for SMB companies
- Be reasonably and quickly communicative with executive oversight personnel if you believe the project is in jeopardy

The project manager's long-term reputation hinges on their success, so most professional project managers are prepared to withdraw if they're not being effective and keeping the project on track. If you've hired a professional project manager and thoroughly checked their references, take it very seriously if they wish to withdraw. I withdraw when I suspect legal or ethical failures of my client or when I clearly see the train coming at me in the tunnel. The technique is my last resort to provide the company managers with a slap alongside the head.

Internal Project Management Despite the Warnings

As a SMB owner or manager, in order to lower the cost of implementation with both internal staff and external consultants, you've decided you're going to do the project management internally. You want a low-cost implementation and you're willing to take the risk. You're a knight who believes his sword has a sharper edge.

But…you must do your homework; otherwise you'll simply ride out in your armor like previous knights to slay the dragon and end up joining the other dead knights that have gone ahead of you. Take the time to devise a different plan.

Process Control with a Task List

Case Study: The Birdhouse Project

I learned project management in the early 1980's from a professor on loan to Portland State University from a blue chip company. He was about to retire so rather than start another big project he didn't want to stick around to finish, he volunteered to finish his last year as a professor on loan. It was a marvelous opportunity for me.

In the class, the professor suggested we tackle a simple project to build a birdhouse. He handed out a one-page instruction sheet that required a "prototype" using cardboard, instructions to create a detailed supply list, and resources recommended for research about the requirements for the type of bird we wanted to attract—all the components of a small project. Fortunately he added at the end, "If you don't want to build a birdhouse, talk to me about alternatives at the end of class." I was just beginning my first evaluation process for a minicomputer accounting system and he was pleased to help me with a real project.

Case Study: The Hand Project

With an implementation in the late 1980's, another former blue chip project manager was engaged as a director on my employer's board. He taught me two things:

1. Sit away from him during board meetings; otherwise I would be constantly removing his hand from my thigh.
2. Keep a simple task plan because anything more complex is unmanageable for anyone except a fulltime, professional project manager whose job is to spew prolific paperwork.

The Task List

I still use an Excel table nearly identical to the task list these two blue chip executives taught me. I used it for this book project. See a sample in Diagram A and on the web in an Excel spreadsheet at www.rapidimplementation.com.

Rapid Implementation Book

Status	Start Date	Due Date	Tasks	Responsibility of	Internal Hours	External Hours
Open	1/2/2013	1/15/2013	eBook Publication contract	Gloria	2	
Open	1/2/2013	1/15/2013	Contract and informatioin from Lightninig Source	Gloria	4	
Open	1/15/2013	2/1/2013	Adobe InDesign / book formatting	Susan		4
Open	12/1/2012	2/1/2013	Formation of a Style Sheet	Susan		2
Open	2/1/2013	2/1/2013	Book artwork, including dustcover	Gloria	4	
Open	2/1/2013	2/1/2013	Book half title i	Gloria	1	
Open	2/1/2013	2/1/2013	Frontispiece-ii	Gloria	1	
Open	2/1/2013	2/1/2013	Title page-iii	Gloria	1	
Open	2/1/2013	2/1/2013	Copyright page-iv	Gloria	1	
Open	2/1/2013	2/1/2013	Table of Contents-vi	Gloria	1	
Open	2/1/2013	2/1/2013	Acknowledgements-vii	Gloria	1	
Open	2/1/2013	2/1/2013	About the Author-end	Gloria	1	
Open	6/1/2012	2/1/2012	The Actual Book	Gloria	450	
Open	2/5/2013	2/10/2013	Editing			32
Open	1/2/2013	2/15/2013	Rapidimplementation.com--shell	Kelly		8
Open	1/2/2013	2/15/2013	Rapidimplementation.com--artwork	Karyn		8
Open	1/2/2013	3/1/2013	Rapidimplementation.com--early chapters	Ron	24	24
					491	78
			Budget		500	100
			Over (under)		9	22

Simplicity makes this project management tool work for SMBs. If you own a company with a concrete 100-hour budget, this is as easy as it gets. When the spreadsheet is kept updated, if the consultant exceeds hours on a scheduled task, it's immediately obvious that time has to be taken from other tasks to stay within budget.

If you're keeping the spreadsheet updated, it'll be quickly obvious if you're falling behind schedule—the first clue your project will exhibit when it's in jeopardy.

Every task is succinctly noted on the task list. I get quirky with it. I don't allow notes on it that cause it to expand past one line of information for each task. If more details are needed, they go on other documentation. My task list is lean and simple.

Gantt Chart

Use a white board, chalk board, or a big piece of paper on the wall to draw a Gantt chart. Don't be above the technique of using a wall, sticky notes, thumb tacks, and yarn to create your Gantt chart. I met with a prospect whose production department had put sheet metal up on the wall then marked off forty-hour weeks for three shifts. They printed labels for each of their jobs and applied those to magnets. Their magnetic schedule wall worked so well they had me research to find if there was a graphic program similar to it.

Of course, if your personnel know how to use Microsoft Project or other project management tools, use those. Just thought I'd mention that tidbit in case you thought I was against the use of professional tools.

Nagging—Otherwise Known as Good Communication and Checking Back

I had a conversation today with my marketing specialist about the grammatical errors in several blog articles. His response was, "I thought you reviewed them when I sent you an email." I'm frequently overwhelmed with too much work to accomplish and too much email to manage in one day.

I pointed out it was one of my major problems to deal with as a project manager. It's not enough to tell someone to do a task. Give them a deadline and just prior to the deadline, check back with them to determine if the task was completed.

You may be very confused if you read in an earlier chapter where I said good people like to work. Remember that's personnel fully committed to the project, and we're being realistic here. If they're your personnel, they will get distracted. They'll need to assist the temporary personnel with information only they know. Or they'll be so committed and working so hard, they'll get tired. When people get tired, they do the easy work not the new, challenging work. So you need a project manager to follow up, nudge, prioritize, communicate, and motivate.

If you ask three people to do the same task—a request worded like, "Would one of you make sure the backup is done tonight"—it's unlikely the task will be done without project management intervention. If you ask three people to do a variety of tasks, the work won't necessarily be completed on time or in the right sequence. A project manager who owns the process and the outcome is needed to check in on everyone and help them prioritize.

I guarantee if you don't create a written schedule, people will misinterpret verbal instructions, the project will start to fail because tasks are deferred. The easy stuff will be completed and the harder work will be deferred. A complex project must be managed or the project will fail.

Weekly Meetings

Another simple but effective project management communication tool I use is a weekly meeting. I require half of my company consultants to meet with me once a week. The other half of the consultants meet with our customer service manager then he meets with me. It's the consultant's job to concisely review their projects—what they've completed in the last week; what they plan to complete in the next week, what's a priority, and if there are any roadblocks. Most importantly, they're encouraged to brag.

In addition we keep track of how many support cases were opened and resolved each week, how many billable hours were booked, and the percentage of project management hours that were booked against consultants' hours.

Little is accomplished during our weekly meetings, but critical tasks are completed for the meeting and after the meeting. So the meeting itself is short and standup; the prep work and follow up are really what I'm after.

In a one-hour, sit-down weekly company meeting, we conduct a cross-training session. Highly structured at first, the company meeting always breaks down into a team building event with a lot of laughter. It's during this time that most of the useful communication occurs. The initial structure of our company meeting gets everyone started; then the joking with the roadblocks and problems starts and that's when the team comes together. If there is no laughter, you've got one stressed out team. Alternatively, if they're so focused on a problem, the laughter will only come with the resolution.

Creating a forum where people are comfortable is a key to facilitating real communication. Hold your meetings regularly and take the pulse every time. I wouldn't recommend crayons and totem poles. A little pizza and beer, root beer sundaes, or a birthday cake go a long way.

One of the best company meetings we had was in February of 2011 which is right in the middle of our busy season. We also had a sequence of family crises that was nearly unbelievable along with months of record-breaking rain in Portland so I ordered a plastic palm tree and sunlamp. One of my employees got a tub, sack of sand, a lawn chair, beer, and margaritas. We held a bring-back-the-sun party and it worked. We had the first clear day of the year that day.

VI. Rocket Through the Clouds

What you'll learn in this chapter:
- *Strategic and financial questions about a new system*
- *System and data security questions*
- *Questions addressing flexibility*
- *Cloud service and deployment options*

Before making decisions about the location, licensing, and maintenance of your business system, you're aware that there are multiple choices. You may be overwhelmed with the choices and issues and have a lot of questions.

Aside from increasing the speed at which you can deploy your business management system if you choose cloud computing, the responsibility for the successful deployment of your hardware and software shifts from you to your hosting provider. However, you probably have reservations about cloud computing and about putting your business management system in the cloud.

Since I'm taking the position in this book that my experience makes me an expert, what follows are my opinions and recommendations. I've displayed the issues, questions, and my answers so you can quickly scan through them, find the information you need, and ignore what you don't think you need.

Strategic Criteria

Tip	Comment on the Tip
Has your business lost its competitive edge?	Perhaps you've allowed your company's business management system to stagnate and are in need of a significant and rapid change. Utilizing a rapidly-deployed new system may provide you with a breakthrough strategy.
Is your company culture receptive to	Some organizations adapt to frequent changes. Others are rooted in the past with owners and employees who are unwilling to adapt to change because what worked in the past is still working, even if marginally.

change?	
Will a new system fit into your business plan?	Mergers, acquisitions, major product line changes, and changes in market penetration should weigh heavily when you assess whether your company should implement a new business management system.
Are there regulatory issues that restrict your business?	Food, chemical, pharmaceutical, nutraceuticals, and medical product manufacturers have stringent regulatory issues with which to comply. With regulations getting more stringent; a new system may be the only reasonable solution.
Do you currently sell online?	Transaction processing speed, integration, and EDI functionality may be important to you in a new system
Will a new system allow you to reach new markets and customers?	This is an excellent goal to set if your new system integrates into a web store that allows you to reach new markets and customers.

Financial Criteria

Tip	Comment on the Tip
How does a new system fit into my budget?	Consider the funding of your system early in your selection project. If you need to arrange financing, ensure that you can get adequate funding before you've used your personnel's time in a selection project.
What about a return on investment goal?	Quantify whether you'll better collect receivables or more accurately pay vendors to save with discounts. Otherwise, it's like playing horseshoes without the stake. Close enough is good, but a ringer is great.
What if my company wants to capitalize the system costs?	Engage your CPA to determine how your deployment and systems costs can best be handled for tax purposes. With correct treatment, deployment costs can be capitalized.

I want to own my software. Is onsite deployment my only option?	Unless you write your own software, you never own it. You own a license to use it. Perpetual licensing simply means you have a license to use it into perpetuity. In addition to the initial cost of perpetual licenses, you'll incur annual software maintenance costs. If you don't pay the annual maintenance, the next time you replace your hardware, you'll have to repurchase the software. With the speed of technology changes, you'll likely want to upgrade every three to five years. Software subscription pricing is set to be less than or equal to perpetual software costs in that timeframe.
What about sales, productivity, and performance goals?	A classic measurement is sales revenue or production volume per employee. Measure your criteria before you implement and set new goals.
Can I reduce inventory and recognize improved cash flow?	Comprehensive distribution modules should allow you to recognize the items that are selling and those that are stagnant.
Can I increase inventory turns and reduce production costs?	You'll be able to set up min/max quantities and economic order quantities that enable better inventory control. Avoid stock outs, manage lot and serial numbers, and avoid allowing inventory expiration dates.

Onsite Deployment Issues

Tip	Comment on the Tip
What about my current investment in infrastructure?	If you already have an adequate environment and your servers are less than a year old, you may be ready to deploy onsite. If you need upgrades to the environment or servers, you should seriously consider hosting.
I have IT staff and want to retain them.	If you have fifty or more users, you need at least part-time IT technical staff.

I want to cut back on my IT staff costs?	As server, device, and workstation monitoring systems have become more functional and inexpensive, IT staff can manage more and more hardware. If you're the owner or financial manager of a company, you'll want to investigate managed services. If you're in an IT department feeling pressure to downsize, you may want to rip this chapter out of the book.
What are managed services?	Managed services may include monitoring of servers, devices, and workstations for signs of failure, providing you or your service provider the opportunity to repair or replace the hardware before total failure. Managed services may also involve remote backup services.
What's the best method to deploy for offsite users?	If you have multiple locations or multiple remote users, purchasing telecommunication lines with enough capacity for both input and output from the server location is particularly expensive for SMBs. You're better off using a Cloud deployment.
What are my options if slow connectivity is my problem?	You probably think that an onsite environment is your only choice; however, virtual desktop deployments can compensate. Virtual desktops in a hosted environment only transmit the screen refresh. If the connection is broken, the computing still continues. The speed of the computing continues as though the work is 100 percent inside of the hosted environment. If connectivity is frequently interrupted or is interrupted for long periods of time, onsite deployment is the practical solution.

Telecommunications Build out Example

If you have multiple locations, purchasing telecommunication lines with enough capacity for both input and output from the server location is particularly expensive for SMBs. Envision a client housing a server at a main office with twenty employees. Five other locations with another forty employees must access that main office.

The main office needs a ten megabyte line just for the employees at that location, plus they need another ten megabytes of speed to accommodate the remote office access. Each of the five locations has five to ten megabyte connections to the main office. The problem is, with only twenty megabytes at the main office, that twenty megabytes caps total access. A remote office with ten megabytes of connectivity can only use two to three megabytes. The overload diminishes everyone's system performance.

This company could drop the extra ten megabytes of connectivity at the main office with all offices linking into a hosted site with scalable quantities of connectivity.

I've seen similar and worse situations. Unfortunately, IT departments will engage in "empire building"—building out infrastructure that they can manage rather than scale back departments and use hosted facilities and managed services. An IT manager at a sixty-restaurant chain built out infrastructure in the main office, including a huge telecommunication line. He also provisioned for custom PCI compliant credit card processing on the internal network.

With considerably less capital investment, the restaurant chain would have provided a better system for their sixty locations if they had built out in a hosted location.

Case Study: Physical Security Issues

No matter how small your company, in order to ensure your servers have a long life and provide a stable system, you have to allocate the space; condition the air for heat, humidity, and dust; supply the power; secure the room; and bring communication lines to it. It's cheaper now to have your hardware hosted rather than construct space the size of even a small closet. A common fallacy is that your server is more secure on your premises.

An employee of a client with Great Plains Software on DOS back in the 1990's called me to assist with recovery of their system. They advised me their server had crashed, the local network company had delivered a replacement, and could I come on site as soon as possible to reload their software. Key to your understanding of this case, I never saw the old server since my previous on site visit months earlier.

The client had reliable backup tapes so it was merely a matter of reloading relevant programs. Back in the good old days, programs had to be loaded into memory on the server in a controlled sequence to optimize use of the memory. It took me about two days to get the new server reloaded, the data restored, and workstations reconfigured. Total, the client was down eight work days.

A week later, the business owner left a voicemail for me and asked if I would provide his insurance company with a letter explaining the negative impact on the business. Because of my financial background, the owner thought I could best write an effective letter so he could receive his business continuation insurance. I recall that I was getting very curious why the owner wasn't available on site during the down time, and for this critical piece of the project, wasn't talking to me directly.

Two weeks later I finally spoke with the owner's wife and asked if she knew what had caused the server to crash. She candidly advised me, "It was probably when it fell off the table we were moving."

Yup…that'll probably do it every time. In a hosted environment—trust me on this one—no one at a hosted location would move an operating server.

Case Study: Another Physical Security Incident

One of our very long term clients had their two servers in a simple open space in their offices. The server with the business management system had been purchased shortly before a major new hardware upgrade was to be released, so one of their engineers purchased a new motherboard about six months after the server was acquired. He thought he could upgrade the server in a year or so with the new board to prolong the life of the server.

One evening the controller was working late; she started an extensive posting routine then went walking down the hall past the server area. She called me on my cell phone because she found the engineer drilling into the computer case. He explained that the new motherboard didn't quite fit so he needed to make a small hole in the case.

We spent several days after that replacing some components because the server crashed badly. For the next server upgrade, the client built out a small room with appropriate power, air conditioning, and a lock.

If engineers and technical staff at a hosted location won't move a live server, drilling into the back of a live server never even occurs to them.

Case Study: Environment Issues

With Microsoft Dynamics products you have multiple choices of where to locate your hardware. Of course you're aware you can keep your hardware at your site. We've worked on servers in many types of structures, rooms, and spaces.

We have one client with a bomb-proof server room. If their building burned to the ground, their server room would fill with a fire suppressant, seal itself off, and drop to the first floor. Theoretically, they could recable to it, replace desktops, and be operative. The style of room was built for use at airports—the rooms that could have a bomb taken to them and detonated with minimal damage to people and structures.

The other end of the spectrum includes a bathroom where my engineers had to sit on a toilet to work at the server, several clients who house their servers in restrooms with slightly better access, one client who used the office shower stall as the server room—they left the showerhead operative—and one client who formerly housed multiple servers in an unfinished basement.

In the unfinished basement, my SQL database engineer and I were working during a heavy rainfall and noticed a trickle of water running across the floor. We were only managing the business management software, not the hardware. Because the servers were setting directly on the floor, we glanced at each other and I immediately said, "We're out of here." The client's resolution to the water problem was to place the servers on wooden pallets.

The only light in the room was in the middle of the room; it was an old-fashioned light with a pull string tied on after the tiny metal bead cord broke. On the next visit after the water problem, I groped for the pull string, tripped on the pallets, and fell into the stack of servers. After that, I always brought a flashlight with me.

The basement was in a historic building. My SQL database engineer and I were there on another evening and joked with each other how fast we'd leave if we felt an earthquake. The discussion undoubtedly was spurred by our unconscious recognition of a small earthquake. Twenty minutes later when we left, the disk jockey on the radio station announced that there had just been a small earthquake whose epicenter was directly beneath our feet. We learned that night what the funky device spanning a crake in the foundation was measuring.

Cloud Service Models

Tip	Comment on the Tip
What is cloud computing?	The definition of cloud computing varies as much as a cloud in the sky. It's better to talk about the components that consist of Infrastructure, Platform, and Software. These are currently referred to as: • Infrastructure as a service (IaaS) • Platform as a Service (PaaS) • Software as a Service (SaaS)
What's covered by IaaS?	IaaS refers to the building, environment, environment controls such as air conditioning and filtering, redundant telecommunication lines, redundant power, and racks. These aspects may also be referred to as ping, pipe, and power.
What's covered by PaaS?	PaaS refers to the servers, routers, switches, drive arrays, and other peripheral equipment. A key component, the backup of your data, may be included in PaaS or SaaS. PaaS may also include the Operating System. I warned you the definitions are fuzzy.
What's covered by SaaS?	SaaS includes all the software starting with the: • Operating System, • Database, and • Microsoft Office applications. Add to this virtually any kind of software: • Customer/Vendor/Member Relationship Management software (XRM software), • Business management system software (sometimes referred to as ERP Software), • Web site software, • Credit card processing software, and • Other business applications. A key component, the backup of your data, may be included in PaaS or SaaS.

Cloud Deployment Models

- Public Cloud
- Community Cloud
- Private Cloud
- Hybrid Cloud

Tip	Comment on the Tip
What is a Public Cloud?	Public Cloud deployment includes all service model components: infrastructure, platform, and software. The application software that you use for XRM (any type of Relationship Management) and your business management system may be deployed on a shared database. This environment is also known as a multitenant environment.
Is my data confidential in the Public Cloud?	The system administration is controlled by your hosting provider, and your data is visible to them. The confidentiality of your data should be protected from other users like you and you're unable to access system administration of the operating system and database; if you can then other users can. If your data must be more highly protected because of its confidentiality, you shouldn't choose Public Cloud computing.
What is a Community Cloud?	A Community Cloud is a multitenant environment where the users have something in common—typically an industry and the same software applications.
Is my data confidential in a Community Cloud?	Security and confidentiality are similar to the circumstances of the Public Cloud. The system administration is controlled by your hosting provider, and your data is visible to them. The confidentiality of your data should be protected from other users like you and you're unable to access system administration of the operating system and database; if you can then other users can. If your data must be more highly protected because of its confidentiality, you shouldn't choose Community Cloud computing.

What is a Private Cloud?	A Private Cloud can have two types of subdeployments: Physical or Virtual
What is a physical Private Cloud?	This environment starts with IaaS—your environment is at a hosted colocation. You own the platform and software within that colocation. You have higher security, more control, and more responsibility with this deployment. This deployment may likely be chosen by companies with high security and confidentiality requirements like medical providers and financial services.
What is a virtual Private Cloud?	This environment includes IaaS and the physical components of PaaS. Your servers are virtual servers deployed on the platform. While you have less control and responsibility with this deployment than a physical deployment, it still meets high security and confidentiality requirements.
Is my data confidential in a Private Cloud?	As you might assume, your data confidentiality is more within your control the more you privatize. Airlines, banks, hospitals, and government agencies use colocations that they own and completely control. As companies move down the spectrum of the need for confidentiality, the next environment is a physical or virtual Private Cloud. This is where you must interject your needs and thoughts to make a choice. You have a high level of confidentiality in a physical Private Cloud. In a virtual Private Cloud, your host's system administrator must deploy your virtual environment. The confidentiality can still be preserved by password protection on a SQL database, for example.

System and Data Security

Electronic security, otherwise known as "Intrusion Detection," is probably higher with IaaS and PaaS service models and cloud deployment methods. Even Private Cloud environments are going to have higher intrusion detection required by the hosting colocation than an onsite deployment.

Hosting colocations that provide IaaS, PaaS, and SaaS service models and any of the deployment models are going to purchase more sophisticated, functional, flexible, and up-to-date intrusion detection applications and hardware than most SMBs.

My experience is that SMBs allow their personnel to have whatever type of mobile device they prefer. Different mobile devices require different technology to connect to your network; each device opens up different access points to intrusion.

In my experience, mobile devices have become the most common point of intrusion, replacing the president's floppy disk drive as the weakest point in the system. I can't recount how many desktop computers we've had to clean after summer, holiday, and spring breaks. But with mobile devices, the crooks can get in anytime. In my opinion, internet and email intrusion detection is much more powerful in Public and Community Cloud deployment. The Cloud is fuzzy; there are millions of entry points. The big email hosts have existed since the 1990's and each hosts hundreds of thousands of users. Your email is much more likely to be captured or damaged while in transit across the cloud than while it's stored on a server.

Tip	Comment on the Tip
What about backup of my data?	State of the art backup is accomplished by streaming your compressed, encrypted data to datacenters for storage. Redundant backups are streamed to a second datacenter hundreds of miles away. Intronis is one company used by large companies and managed service providers for backup purposes.
With mobile devices, what's the better service model?	Email is notorious for intrusion. Companies of all sizes use hosted email for security concerns alone. You remove the threat from the remainder of your system. The biggest threat is while the email message and its attachments are intransit through the cloud. My opinion is: hosted email is more secure.
I'm not convinced, is there a secure email service?	Yes, encrypted email services from www.n-krypt.com

Hosted Physical Security

Security involves physical and electronic access to your systems and data. The confidentiality of your systems and data may be higher onsite or in a Private Cloud, but the physical security is probably much lower onsite in an SMB than in any type of hosted deployment. Starting with the approach and outside of most host locations, these physical attributes far exceed physical security for most SMBs. We derived the following list from our host provider, ViaWest.

Tip	Comment on the Tip
Is the area fenced?	Indicates a considerably higher level of security
Is there restricted gate access?	Indicates a considerably higher level of security
Is there a vehicle trap?	Indicates a considerably higher level of security. After personnel pass through the first gate, it closes, the second gate doesn't open until the first gate is closed, and neither gate opens unless personnel have appropriate access.
Is access to the building monitored?	All hosting colocations will be monitored. Are there cameras or just people? Are the people supplemented by motion detectors that catch their attention?
Is access to the spaces housing equipment monitored?	Are there cameras or just people? Are the people supplemented by motion detectors that catch their attention? Are there keypad and passcard controls and how sophisticated are they?
Is there a man trap?	Indicates a considerably higher level of security. After personnel pass through the first door, it closes, the second door doesn't open until the first door is closed, and neither door opens unless personnel have appropriate access.
Are there redundant services?	Learn about power, environment conditioning, fuel supplies, telecommunication lines, and redundancy associated with maintaining the building and equipment.

How does the facility screen personnel?	Develop an understanding of how they screen and hire personnel.
Does the facility provide copies of their audit reports?	Some of the ranking methods for security and procedures of hosted sites are compliance certifications and audits termed SSAE 16 Type II SOC 1 Report, SOC 3 Report, and PCI Report on Compliance for Sections 9 and 12. Under nondisclosure agreements, the hosting colocation should be willing to provide you with a copy of their audit report.

Case Study: Hosted Site Security Evaluation

My engineers were initially excited about using one particular host site which we toured. I noted the site camera fixed on the back door, but that no one was really watching the feed from that camera. I was advised the server room was restricted by card key access. While we were left alone during the tour (which is a problem by itself), I went out the back door, allowed it to close, and then slipped my credit card between the door jam and lock to open the door. As I came inside, I just looked at my engineers and shook my head. No one at the host site said anything to me; no one had noticed what I had done.

A frequently-used cliché most people inaccurately attribute to Supreme Court Justice Potter Stewart (1915 – 1985) when he described his criteria for pornography: "I know it when I see it." Good security should be obvious during site visits.

Flexibility

As you realize, the Public Cloud allows you to deploy most rapidly, but you must question if that's the right long-term choice for you. SMBs should consider multiple flexibility issues:

Tip	Comment on the Tip
Am I forced into upgrades in a Public Cloud?	Fundamentally, in a Public Cloud the answer is "Yes." Upgrades of the platform and application software are services made a part of your monthly subscription fee. Insure you understand how much notice you'll receive so you can adequately prepare.
Am I forced into upgrades in a Community Cloud?	You'll likely with feel less stress with upgrades and your business processes in a Community Cloud if the driving force behind the Community is application software. For instance, ISVs developing industry-specific software that integrates to core Microsoft Dynamics® GP financial modules have six months to upgrade their software to make it compatible with newly released versions of Dynamics GP to maintain their preferred status with Microsoft. If you join a Community Cloud driven by the ISV, they will likely prototype the upgrade and provide you with more notice than if you were in a Public Cloud environment.
Does a Cloud environment eliminate the possibility of using custom software?	Some Cloud environments preclude the ability to use customizations. These types of software are termed "configurable" rather than customizable. Both the use of software from ISVs and customized software may influence whether you choose Public, Community, Private, or Hybrid Cloud deployments. Private environments don't typically restrict you. Hybrid Cloud deployments must be investigated individually for that functionality.
Will company growth affect my choice of Service or Deployment models?	Depending on the hosted software, company growth will affect your choice. Entry-level software applications aren't any more stable on a host system than on a server by your desk. The underlying issue is the caliber of the underlying database and application logic. Going from one to ten to twenty five users is a big issue for a database.
If I'm limited on the addition of customizations and ISV Software, what are my options?	Look for hosts that support your ISV Software. If you contact the ISV directly, they'll likely be able to direct you to a host that provides subscription licenses of their software. Within a Private Cloud, you aren't restricted from customizations or ISV Software.

What if I miss the mark on my choice of vendors and want to move my system?	Do your homework choosing your host in the beginning to determine how cooperative they'll be moving your system. The better the host, the more confident they are, and the more communicative and cooperative they'll be explaining your options. If the infrastructure and platform host is separate from the subscription software, you simply find a new infrastructure and platform host. If the host and the software developer are the same, and they absolutely do not sell perpetual licenses or work through partners for hosting, you won't be able to move.
What about deployment tools and options?	Transition, integration, and configuration tools and services are vital for a rapid implementation. Develop an understanding of what is available.
What about deployment services?	Professional consultants, integration specialists, trainers, and support personnel are vital to your success. Insure that a network of organizations and personnel are widely available to you.
What are my training alternatives?	Training methodology differs with each software developer and consultant organization. Look for online webinars and training manuals from the software developer. Your consultants should be able to provide classroom, onsite, and custom training.
What about post implementation integration and reporting tools?	Midmarket software is most commonly, although not exclusively, provided based on Microsoft SQL. Microsoft SQL Server Integration Services (SSIS) and SQL Server Reporting Services (SSRS) are powerful, flexible, and widely used.
What about other custom reporting tools with which I'm more familiar?	Microsoft Access, Excel, and Word; Crystal Reports, and any reporting tool with ODBC connectivity can be used with products using Microsoft SQL Server. With Microsoft Dynamics products there are ISV products for custom reporting: Jet Reports and Solver, for example.
What about financial statements?	The financial statement report writer will be embedded within or tightly integrated to your business management system. Microsoft provides Management Reporter integrated with its Dynamics products.

Does your host software developer have a marketplace of third-party products?	A large following of third-party products is an endorsement of the core product. Rather than customizing the system to meet your specialized needs, you may well accelerate your implementation in addition to stabilizing it and lowering your costs with a widely-supported third-party product.

VII. Software Licensing

What you'll learn in this chapter:
- *Named and concurrent user licensing*
- *Device licensing*
- *Perpetual and subscription licensing*

There are two characteristics of software licensing to understand. First of all, licenses are sold on an access basis: named user licenses, concurrent user licenses, or device licenses. Named user licenses are attached to Windows Active Directory (AD). Every AD user requires a separate license even if all users aren't logged onto the system at the same time.

Concurrent licenses provide for a certain number of users to log on at any one time. Concurrent user licenses tend to be more expensive than named user licenses.

Device licenses specify how many devices can access a server; for example, mobile bar code devices accessing a server.

Then we deal with whether the software license is on a perpetual or subscription basis. Perpetual licenses provide for the right to use the software into perpetuity; however, there is usually an annual maintenance fee. Microsoft perpetual licenses are generally supported for five years after the initial release date, although exceptions are made for support beyond five years.

Subscription licenses are purchased on a monthly basis. Most hosted systems use subscription licenses. Five years, sixty months, of monthly subscription licenses cost approximately the same as a perpetual license plus five years of software maintenance. If you're trying to avoid the large, upfront expenditure, the subscription license is a better choice.

VIII. Swim with Your Software Vendor without Getting Stung

At one point in my business career, I met an associate who told me this version of a story about a frog and a scorpion. I've heard many versions of it since, so it's not attributable to any one person.

A scorpion lived on an island. A frog in the river became friends with the scorpion, but was careful to maintain his distance. When a forest fire started to engulf the island, the scorpion convinced the frog to ferry him off the island, assuring the frog he wouldn't be stung; after all, he pointed out, if he stung the frog, they would both die. The frog was convinced the scorpion wouldn't sting him so he agreed to ferry the scorpion to safety across the river. As he neared the shore, the scorpion stung him. As they both sank to their death, the frog asked, "Why did you do that? You promised me you wouldn't sting me."

The scorpion explained, "I had to sting you. It's my nature."

What you'll learn in this chapter:
- *The book and the chapter aren't a competitive analysis*
- *The nature of the market*
- *The vendor's competitive environment and how it influences quotes and estimates*
- *How to maintain control of your selection process*

I'm not Writing a Competitive Analysis

A competitive analysis of software vendors or even software developers isn't within the scope of this book. Competitive analysis of approximately 4,000 business management system products and the hundreds of thousands of consultants who support them is a company mission. Not mine.

I mention a number of software developers within the book, but that isn't the point. I use them as examples because they're the top names and I maintain my familiarity with them; specifically, I'm deeply familiar with

Microsoft Dynamics® GP. Except when it gets to the technical chapters for Dynamics GP, this book could be used for any product. I do go into explicit details about Dynamics GP in Chapter XIX.

The Fuzzy Factors and Nature of the Market

I've already discussed the selection of your vendor in the prior chapter providing you with all the rational, logical, technical steps to take to assess your vendor. There are always a number of other factors involved in a selection process which are fuzzy factors.

I first met a respected, local consultant in 1990 shortly after deciding to become a Great Plains Software consultant. His early assessment of me, "You might have an angle because you've been a buyer not a salesperson, but I recommend you get out of this industry as fast as you can."

I introduced myself to him again last fall after his presentation at a local professional group and started to remind him of what he'd told me. He cut me off before I finished, "Yes, I remember. You didn't listen to me! Good! Look where you are today."

I started out in this industry as a buyer and user of systems and still consider myself more of a frog than a scorpion. If I were a buyer again, the following are the things that I've learned the hard way about this market. My hope is to reinforce what you already know and maybe provide a glint of enlightenment.

Sales and Distribution Channels

Some of the biggest, most successful software development companies in the world employ a trained sales force to sell software. That's called a direct sales channel. These organizations are big on cultivating, training, and growing their sales employees.

Other big, successful software developments sell through distributors and resellers. That's an indirect sales channel. These organizations are big on cultivating, training, and growing their partners.

There are also retail sales channels. I'm sure you could dissect the market more and get into details, but that's enough here.

Microsoft, Oracle, Sage, and NetSuite use all those sales channels, and they insure it is a well-trained sales force whether it's a person directly employed by them for enterprise sales, a reseller for SMBs, or their retail stores. These organizations are big, effective marketing and sales machines. Their nature is to sell to you.

Market competition is heating up. Intuit is pushing upwards with QuickBooks; NetSuite is claiming a share of the midmarket. Oracle is pushing itself downward in the market. The six products in the Microsoft Dynamics product line are pushing up, down, and sideways in the market. Sage just announced that support for MAS 500 will cease in five years so it's pushing clients towards Sage X3.

The point is that these developers need ever-increasing sales revenue to maintain their competitive edge. For the most part, the market is demanding newer versions of software constantly. Microsoft and other operating system developers push this somewhat, but even Microsoft is being pushed by the hardware manufacturers all the way back to chip manufacturers and how fast their chips process. The market is following smart phone technology by moving to touch screens.

Business management software is at the starting edge of a new generation of web-based, subscription-based software licensing. This new generation of software requires millions of dollars of investment, research, and development. Google, Amazon, and countless others have pulled the market onto the Internet and it takes a whole bundle of money to fund the research and development to keep up.

So you better be prepared to be in multiple sales funnels the moment you start searching for anything to do with ERP or business management software. A vendor knows you're there before you move to the next site. I get emails daily with a list of who's been on our sites—the company name and contact names of who was likely looking at our site.

Monitoring software on the web is so sophisticated a third party can watch who is hitting another company's web site (and this is legal, by the way). So if you log onto a particular software developer's web site, a list collector can see that happen and start to work backwards from your IP address to identify who the likely contact is at your company that's interested in business management software. In addition to the emails I receive about who is looking at our site, I get a dozen emails a day from list collectors trying to sell me a list of who is using Dynamics.

If you think you're being inconspicuous because you're merrily inputting notafrog@fakemail.com, or your name and phone number is Brown Toad at 123-456-7890, or you're implementing DIY, you're actually already deep into the vendor's sales funnel. Using fake contact information is nearly useless.

Facilitating your ability to start your implementation on your own is just a very cheap marketing method. Don't think it's all clever marketing though. It meets the needs of many SMB companies.

Sales Methods

The sales methodology, by any name, that has proven to be the most effective is designed to:

- Gain your trust
- Get to know your decision makers
- Understand your decision-making process
- Determine the problems with your existing system
- Emotionally amplify the problems deep and wide across your organization
- Create a vision of their software solving your problems
- Lead you through a decision-making process to choose the salesperson's software

You maintain control by going back to Chapter II and completing the steps in that chapter. Put the effort into written strategic criteria and other documentation and processes you've defined and you'll have a lesser feeling of being "sold."

- If the reseller only focuses on your problems, that's a clear sign they're trying to manipulate you.
- If they attempt to magnify your problems across the organization, they're trying to manipulate you.
- If they insist that a discount is a onetime deal, it never is. You know this is the most common pressure tactic. I personally hate discounts. When you compare the cost of the software versus the total cost of the implementation, the discount pales. Ignore it until you're truly ready to buy.

Occasionally discounts are significant. In 2009, Microsoft released a promotion "Three Users For A Buck." I had four small sales pending at nearly full price and one small sale I had just completed. A local competitor advised my new client of the promotion because they didn't know I had already closed the sale (or maybe it was retribution). That was a difficult conversation because Microsoft isn't a mattress store with refunds for future discounts. I stepped forward to close all four sales at the new promotion price, losing an estimated $40,000 in profit.

To determine if a discount is truly advantageous to you, you must be absolutely certain you're choosing the right software and the discount must be substantial enough to offset your cost of funds to warrant accelerating your purchase timeframe.

If you follow a selection process, each step will be countered, facilitated, or diminished by different sales tactics in use by the reseller. In the initial phase, they'll qualify you just as much as you'll qualify them. Experienced resellers, honest or manipulative, will almost immediately qualify you on five points:

1. What is your timeframe?
2. Who makes the decision to buy?

3. What general kind of system are you looking for?
4. How large is your company in terms of gross revenue, number of employees, or size and number of transactions?
5. What is your budget?

It's just like being qualified by the car salesman. If he shows you what you want at the price you can afford, will you buy today? If you're just browsing he'll leave you alone and periodically check back with you if he has time. A good software salesperson must do the same thing to save you from wasting your time, and, of course, save their time.

If someone isn't open to telling me their budget, I'll watch the body language while I step through, "Is $25,000 too much? Is $50,000 too much?" I keep going until I see them wince; then I go backward to their comfort zone and tell them what we can do inside their budget.

Early in my career I tip toed around these questions, not willing to offend anyone. In 2013, I find out who the decision makers are and the size of the company before I talk with the initial contact person the first time. If they won't answer the other questions, I'll attempt to negotiate an exchange for an introduction to the decision makers. If I don't get the answers I need, I put them into our nurture campaign.

I have found out there's no faster way to motivate someone to jump back into my sales funnel than to tell them they can't afford my software, but that never works out in the end so I don't use it as a sales tactic.

One manipulative tactic I've seen used was extremely effective for that salesperson. If the prospect or client wasn't listening to him and he believed their implementation was going to fail, he would simply state the obvious, "You're not listening to me and this is going to be a train wreck. We can't help you." He would immediately leave—no goodbyes or handshakes. He would simply walk out. He made it clear to his employees they weren't supposed to say a thing. As quickly as they could, they were to pick up their belongings, not look back, and leave with him. He told me he always regained control within forty-eight hours.

The Sting of the Sales Quote

The biggest issue with IT projects: they run over budget and timeframe. Three reasons cause this:

1. The project isn't scoped accurately in the first place because the reseller must bring in a competitive, but usually inaccurate quote to win the business.
2. The project isn't scoped accurately in the first place because the needs analysis and project plan weren't completed accurately in advance.
3. The project isn't scoped accurately due to a force majeure—something no one thought could possibly happen did happen.

Every buyer and seller in the marketplace under scopes IT projects. When have you seen these headlines?

- Bridge project two million dollars under budget
- Water treatment plant completed under budget

Okay. So everyone knows that. What's going with the competitive problem? A competitive product in my industry is so well known for undercutting, counteracting it has become an art form. We know they are going to underbid services, so to remain competitive, one choice we have is to also underbid. Darn! I hate being dishonest.

Instead we do our best to provide details why our services are higher. Our product isn't harder to learn. Legacy data doesn't change depending upon what system it's being pushed into; in fact, we usually have an advantage with legacy data because of toolset and expertise. Our hourly rates are generally slightly less than our local competitors' rates and substantially less than national organizations' rates. Comparable products, modules, functionality, and reports are generally quoted. Our challenge is to present information that explains the difference.

In my opinion a detailed discussion of the process usually reveals the discrepancy. Sales Order Processing personnel generally need four hours of training. So the quote lists four hours, right? Wrong! The needs analysis reveals five locations with four to twenty personnel at each location. No one transports their whole sales force offsite for a half day of training. Transportation time and lunch…the day is gone. So the training schedule shows the multiple classes, the cost of bringing the instructor to the salespeople. And the fact that salespeople are terrible students who always have a good reason to skip class so there's a few makeup classes at the end.

We go through a similar analysis with the integration of legacy data. See your alternatives in Chapter XVI. We just keep going down the list of actions until we prove our point. Or we lose the deal.

This one happens all the time: The owner wants competitive bids and gets involved in the process long enough to get two or three equal bids. We know one competitor is going to send an impressive sales executive in at the end to offer a discount if the owner signs "Right Now!" which is always timed to be the last moment before the sales executive has to leave to catch his plane. Running out of time to negotiate is very effective.

We counteract this by holding back on our discount until the end. We advise our champion if the other guy drops his pants at the last minute, we will if the champion can prove it by showing us the bid. The buyer always wins this one but it's risky for the buyer because he may not get all the services he needs. If he doesn't have the authority later in the project to sign a change order, it's risky. You get what you pay for.

Alternatively, we have a champion with budget override authority. The owner accepts the champion's recommendation, signs off on the competitive bid; the champion pitches in later with a change order.

I was in a situation to assist a client to negotiate the purchase of a new minicomputer and was asked to hold back on the cost of a system the company could not afford. Plain and simple in my opinion, they should have purchased something at one-tenth the cost. I found out later the owner knowingly pitted the purchasing agent and I against one another. It didn't work.

To get the system the purchasing agent wanted at the price I wanted (which I still thought was way too much), the salesperson cut modules out of the initial purchase. After the initial $200,000 was spent, the purchasing agent pointed out to the owner that amount was non-recoverable sunk cost. To get what the company needed, the owner needed to put in another $50,000. The ploy worked.

Don't give away needed functionality to stay within your budget. Highly question when consulting costs vary considerably between competitive quotes. Check the references carefully for the company with the lower quote. You may find the reference customer felt training was substantially lacking or they issued material change orders simply because the vendor's quote was a lowball.

Maintain Control of Your Selection Process

You and I tend to do business with people we like. I personally have devoted so many years and hours to my business, I want to be working with people I enjoy. To be an enjoyable, successful business relationship hinged upon the implementation of a significant product like a business management system, the vision must be created of successful operation of the product, and the vision must ultimately be fulfilled. Vendors go about creating that vision of success in various ways.

Avoiding the business relationship gives you a false sense of control. Arm yourself with information about how the selection and buying process works so you have more confidence to obtain the kind of help you need and want.

Especially with a cloud solution, you may be pushing back right now thinking you don't need a business relationship. In fact, you want to initially avoid salesperson or consulting contact. You sign up for that NetSuite account and start setting up your system. Or better yet, you find one of those 30-days-free Microsoft Dynamics hosts. In either case, you never make or take a phone call when you start.

I venture that's one of the leading causes of churn in the cloud market. You don't want to "be sold" so you avoid the salesperson. You don't want expensive services, so you avoid the consultant completely. You view the developer, value added reseller, and consultant as adversaries.

An understanding of the reasons behind the behavior of vendors will enable you to maintain control of your selection and implementation processes. Do your homework. If you develop a functional requirements list that includes both the functions that your current system does well and the additional or different functionality that you want, you can stick to that list when evaluating the software. That will prevent the vendor from focusing on only the functions that their software does extremely well and keep them away from intensifying the current problems.

Traits of a Trustworthy Vendor

Most likely a value-added reseller for an SMB will have a project plan used numerous times for successful small company implementations.

They'll expect to initially meet the champion (the person who wants a new system the most), but they'll immediately work towards saving you and themselves some time by determining who is on the selection committee, who influences the decision, and who makes the final decision.

They'll ask key questions from everyone they speak to within your company. Sixty percent or more of their sales time will be spent listening to you. If they start selling too soon, push back.

Some of my most effective clients have outright hung up on salespeople or cut meetings short and asked the salesperson to leave when there's too much selling and not enough listening. Tribal governments and casinos in the last ten to fifteen years have made many large purchases of software and systems. They've learned to follow processes, especially with demonstrations and prototypes.

Case Study: A Fake Demonstration

Before the vendor demonstrates software, they should perform an analysis of your needs related to their software. If your strategic needs and functional requirements aren't documented and the vendor is a specialist in your industry, they may step up very quickly with a demonstration based on what they know you should want. In my opinion, this is a mistake on their part and your part.

The combination of your team and company, the implementation consultants, and the software (which is changing every quarter) is unique for every implementation.

One of my clients made a million dollar mistake with a software product unique to their industry. They did all the right things, following a sound, documented selection process complete with detailed functional requirements. They didn't realize the demonstration was actually a PowerPoint capture of the software which was only in its design phase. With highly-scripted fake clicks, the vendor successfully convinced the buyers they were viewing operational software. The buyers didn't throw a left curve into the demonstration.

You'll want and need a ballpark estimate before you move forward with the actual purchase of software, before the prototype, and before you make a final choice on the reseller. Your ballpark estimate should be accompanied by a project plan; we use Microsoft Project to prepare a Gantt chart. Pay close attention to training time, integration time, report writing, and customizations. See the relevant chapters on these processes.

- Training time—Chapter XVI
- Integration time—Chapters XV, XVII, XVIII
- Report writing—Chapters XX and XXI
- Customizations— Chapter XXVI

I dread when a customer wants to implement on their own unless I perceive they're the 1 in 100 competent enough to be successful. I don't mind the lost revenue if they succeed; I truly enjoy working with extremely competent clients. I'm sad though because I rarely lose revenue when a customer decides to implement on their own. I usually end up earning more revenue because first I have to tear down the mess they've created then I have to reconstruct the system. But I dread earning a living doing cleanup!

Common Software Selection Processes

Typically, we encounter companies starting their search process with these alternative approaches:

- An executive or team with the authorization to do so engages an objective consultant to assist them with creating an RFI (Request for Information. This is a highly-respected first step for large companies.
- An executive gathers a team together and produces a more casual document listing their needs.
- I've encountered public companies with needs written on a few sheets of yellow paper.
- I've encountered countless SMBs, midmarket, and public companies that start their process talking to several Resellers, repeating their problems over and over. The price of the software and the first ballpark estimate of the cost of the project are major determinants of who the project stakeholders decide to continue to talk with.

In all cases, the prospective client will likely receive back:

- Sales positioning documents assuring them the software vendor has heard their pain and can resolve the problems
- Substantiation of vendor claims based on fact sheets
- Demonstrations of vendor prowess with the software solving their problems
- Case studies and references from happy customers

- A fixed-fee quote or an estimate of cost, always more than the prospect wanted or perceived was necessary

There's always a discount with a deadline that urges you to make a choice between vendors and products before you're truly prepared.

Many individuals in SMB companies start their search for a business management product by looking outward at vendors and products. They want to find the best product to fit their needs and a good deal provided by a software vendor who has implemented in their industry previously.

Other individuals perceive they're starting a project out correctly by mapping their needs. In reality, they're usually just listing their pains and problems. If they do detail their needs well, they still haven't addressed the many areas of the project that will cause them cost overruns, in my opinion.

Case Study: Food Manufacturing Company

In a food manufacturing company, the client broke their legacy system by failing to upgrade it for 20 years while the company grew five fold. While we were assured by the client that they could quickly and easily extract their inventory item information, their real inventory items were contained in silos of information gathered with manual processes and Excel worksheets.

Their about-to-be ex-consultant and my personnel extracted data, but about eighty percent of it was obsolete. All but the financial modules of the legacy software system had been abandoned by the users years ago.

The real data was virtually inaccessible because it was stored in the countless Excel worksheets and manual processes across the organization. Others who needed the same information for a different purpose created their own data, but naturally it was never identical. The real system had become a quagmire of complex manual processes to use the same data multiple times.

Nearly every quote was created initially in Excel, with no sales management process review, success/failure statistics, or management control over margins. Big wins got attention, but the system was so broken, it was impossible to determine if the profit margin was reasonable without a lot of review of standalone Excel worksheets.

Diving down into this implementation revealed the client not only needed an business management system implementation, they needed process design, intensive data gathering and transformation, management reporting design, and much more extensive user training than initially quoted.

User training was a process of breaking old habits and teaching new processes. System design was a balancing act between creating small customizations versus using functionality the system already provided in a slightly different format. Users depended upon their unique processes to win sales and were reluctant to move to a collaborative, more efficient system.

Case Study: Competitive Quote for a Financial Company

I had encountered and lost to our competitors previously so I knew what positioning they would take and how I would counter balance it. The CFO became our champion within a large team of division managers, stating, "I think your team is the one to get us through this." But we had to produce a quote for the owners and managers comparable to our competitors. The competitors had quoted an implementation where they were on site two weeks then everything else they did was remote.

I knew a two-week implementation was ridiculous for this company; the CFO knew that process had previously failed when the company was smaller, so he and I agreed we would be available as long as the company needed us (within reason because I won't live forever). We were local so that was an advantage. We produced a quote with a lower software cost, higher services cost, and a total comparable to the competitor.

IX. A Square Egg

What you'll learn in this chapter
- *How to determine if someone is resistant to an implementation*
- *How to deal with a holdout*

I always look for the holdout during my initial site visits. Who was scheduled to attend the meeting and didn't. Maybe they sit apart from the main group or it could be as simple as they just don't engage in the conversation.

Case Study: The Unique Holdout

One of the unique holdouts I encountered simply left the room anytime I asked him a direct question about decisions with set up options. He always had an urgent phone call to make or email to send. This fellow just had problems making decisions. He created three charts of accounts designs and couldn't choose one. When it became obvious that we weren't going to meet a firm deadline for the Go Live, the project team instructed me to obtain further decisions from the holdout's subordinate, the accounting manager. She understood the company and procedures quite well and is one of my strongest client users today.

Case Study: The Competent Holdout

I once implemented a chemical batch processing system, and had an extremely competent employee refusing to take part. Because she was the retired president's daughter, her job was secure. Approximately two months after the Go Live, I found her in a file room with a stack of the fifth copy of our printed invoices and asked what she was doing with them. She explained she was filing them for me.

"But I never knew there were copies filed back here. I've never looked at these files for a year." I reviewed the invoices which were older than a year and realized the previous controller had been manually marking them up with payment information—information that was now readily available in the new system. So I advised the employee she could stop filing the fifth copy; destroy it until the next print run when we would stop printing so many copies.

Without four hours per day of filing, the PR/HR director realized he could drop my clerk's job from full-time to part-time. The clerk wasn't dismayed at the loss of income; she used the opportunity to return to college.

However, very good employees who are eager to use a new system may hold back on their participation because of the fear of job loss. Each case should be handled with care and consideration with the best resolution being to reassure them of their value if they jump into the project with all their effort and become a champion. They'll be ahead of everyone else, in line for a pay increase and more assured than others of the security of their position.

Case Study: Company Policies May be the Holdout

Holdouts may be as simple as a slow employee. In 1998, I installed a system for a client with a long-term employee who had chosen not to retire. Health problems prevented him from effectively doing his job, but company practices dictated that he not be discharged. All I could offer was additional training to try to bring the employee up to speed.

I admire a company that retains employees with family or medical problems. Accommodation is necessary, appropriate, and legally required. The hard decision comes when the job just simply isn't getting done. I estimate the company lost tens of thousands of dollars in lost vendor discounts and incurred $5,000 to $10,000 in additional training costs. The CFO spent countless hours reconciling inventory and accounts payable because Larry just simply didn't want to use purchase order receiving.

Case Study: The Reluctant Controller

The reluctant controller had a complete system in Microsoft Excel–complex spreadsheets in which he had re-entered all transactions in detail. This company was a puzzling situation; they had two different versions of a competitive mid-market software program. Neither version integrated with each other. One was an obsolete DOS version and the other was an obsolete Windows version. One branch office used an entry-level program. Every transaction from every system was manually re-entered by the reluctant controller into his spreadsheets.

The controller was obviously intelligent and adept with computers. His Excel system was amazingly complex. We just couldn't determine why he created it instead of using the financial module in the Windows version of the midmarket software program. He had meticulously entered all sales and payables entries in his Excel worksheet, linked it to a general ledger worksheet, and produced financial statements in additional linked worksheets.

This duplicate entry was time consuming and expensive for this company—an expense they had overlooked for years, but its lack of effectiveness came to hurt them substantially. The "system" failed to produce the needed financial analysis to reveal that a branch manager was ordering expensive technical equipment and not processing the sale through the company. An effective system would have quickly shown that cost of goods sold was out of proportion to sales or that inventory on hand was excessive.

The controller planned to retire after the implementation; he had agreed to learn the new system so he could assist with the design. Then the client planned a six-month transfer of knowledge to train the new controller who was the fulltime project manager. However, the reluctant controller exhibited such outrageous behavior during training he was distracting to the other students.

He was in and out of class so much he was disruptive. When we asked him to leave only during breaks, he started sighing loudly and frequently, leaning his head on his left arm, and typing only with the middle finger of his right hand. I picked up quickly on the message.

I brought the behavior to the attention of the president and requested that the former controller be omitted from training. All parties were happy with this resolution.

The controller doing double entry contributed to the loss of approximately $200,000 in stolen equipment because of his reluctance to undergo change. Fortunately because he was removed from the project team, the implementation was a success.

Case Study: Mary

My most resistant-to-change client didn't attend the first meeting until we were breaking up the meeting. Then she hesitantly appeared explaining how busy she was that afternoon; she had no doubt been within listening distance where she could hear the tone of the meeting change. There were six of us in the conference room–a fully equipped conference room with audio/visual equipment, a projection screen that descended from the ceiling, an enormous old highly-polished conference table that could seat twenty easily. We were all seated at one end. When Mary joined us, she sat by the door at the other end.

She proceeded for the next four months to avoid every meeting and training session. I was assured her input to decisions wasn't critical and, if they needed to they would schedule one-on-one training for her. The day before her class we had a pleasant chat about what I'd cover the next day.

At 8:00 a.m. the next morning as I was preparing to leave for the client office, I received the call I'll never forget. Mary had died during the night from heart failure. I was assured she had a weak heart for years....but, yeah, the stress killed her. I'm not suggesting better management could have prevented Mary's death, but it just illustrates that some personnel get really stressed from change. We did and said everything reasonably possible to assuage her fears.

Case Study: Retirement Pending

I withdrew from competition for a state agency implementation in 2004 because a key employee was retiring. The agency personnel were concentrating the software selection on HR/PR (Human Resource and Payroll) module attributes, but the HR/PR department manager wasn't at the start of our meeting. Eventually she rushed in late and added that she only had twenty minutes before her next appointment.

My engineer, much more familiar with state agencies, whispered to me, "She probably has a birthday party to attend." For a moment, I couldn't believe that someone would prioritize like that.

We left shortly after her departure, walking past the lunchroom where we spotted the birthday party in progress. The HR/PR manager saw us leaving and stepped out of the room to walk us to the elevator. While I thought that was a nice gesture on her part, sort of an apology for the priorities she had set, she advised me to stop wasting my time; there was no way she was going to implement a new system in the eighteen months prior to her retirement after using a paper based system for nearly thirty years. I suggested to her it would be a nice gesture for her to leave a better system behind for her successor, but that clearly wasn't her goal.

The information manager leading the software selection continued to contact me. I didn't disclose the conversation with the HR/PR manager—I was certain she would deny what she had told me. I assisted him long enough to not burn any bridges and provided him with a needed third bid to meet state requirements, but there was no way we would engage on that project.

I keep quarters at my desk to make bets with employees from time to time. Do you want to bet who won that situation when I checked on them a year later?

Case Studies: Three Failures – Graphic Design and Printing

After a company had purchased software from another reseller and failed at their first implementation, they contacted me. I probably have fifty stories that could start with that sentence.

The company's controller had a goal of low implementation costs. She would achieve this through use of only my training and post-implementation troubleshooting. She would do the design, data import, and document design herself.

This was one of my first implementations of Great Plains Accounting in the 1990's. The controller was willing to spend a little more money working with me than with her first installer. We jointly created a project plan and committed to stick to it. Back then, Great Plains had a total of fourteen modules with a fraction of the current complexity of Microsoft Dynamics® GP. It was quite possible to implement one module at a time. So we planned on a module a month.

On my second visit, I noticed "the bump" (knowing even at this early stage of my career what was highly likely going to happen regarding the implementation) and said, "Oh, you're pregnant. When are you due?" Of course, not coincidentally I've found after twenty three years as a reseller, the due date is always shortly after the Go Live date. There is never any slack time allocated for a delay.

In twenty three years of implementing I have never had an on time and implementation when a key player is pregnant with a due date within two months of the Go Live date. The baby is early, the Go Live gets deferred until unreasonably close to the due date, concentration wanes, or complications arise—pick one or all four. The implementation falters.

Good luck controlling that one though. In this case, the baby arrived early and the project was cancelled until further notice. That was my first failure with this company and their second failure.

The same company about a year later; same budget because the budget wasn't wrong, the baby was early. However, I didn't think to ask this time because I thought, "Who in the world would try this a second time, trying to squeeze another implementation in before a baby's birth." She thought she could pick up where she left off and had allotted even less time until her second child's due date than the first time around.

I would explain my third attempt at this implementation, but you can probably guess the outcome. I was asked again to implement, and I confess, I tried again after verifying she planned no further children. Accidents happen.

The problem isn't the babies. That's just life. The problem was this employee had no management supervision of the project and no ability to control her use of time. The project failed for my third time, her fourth. If she had been allowed to commit her time to the projects, she well could have completed them on time.

Eventually, the company did successfully implement after they hired a different controller. I pushed through to talk with the company president and laid down laws about allocating personnel resources.

Summary

Holdouts may be as simple as a slow employee or one of your most competent employees. The Unique Holdout cost his company 200 hours of additional consulting time – at my rates that's $30,000. The Reluctant Controller doing double entry was responsible for approximately $200,000 of stolen equipment because of the lack of an integrated system that he should have demanded be replaced much sooner. The most heartbreaking holdout just sticks with me as an unfortunate situation.

Recognition of the problem is the first step in effectively dealing with someone who is afraid of the change, the learning curve, or any aspect of the project. I won't pretend that I'm an industrial psychologist and provide you with a lot of ideas of how to deal with people who are difficult in a particular situation. I simply see the results, or lack of results, when someone's not a good fit in a position. I'm just not the kind of person that sweeps problems under the rug and hopes for the best. In that regard, I guess I'm a fixer. Sometimes I'm an in-your-face fixer—I don't shy away from confrontations when there's a problem.

I recommend dealing with the situation so the individual person is appropriately assisted and the company gets the resolution it needs. Choosing set up options is primarily a decision-making process. So put someone in charge that knows the company and is willing to make decisions. If someone is not a good fit in a situation or a position, find someone who is a good fit so everybody is happy.

Deal with indecision, fear of change, and reluctance for any reason before your project starts. One key person with bad attitude or lack of skills can fail or severely compromise a project. Put your energy into resolving the problem before wasting resources on an implementation doomed to fail.

The elephant in the room is the fear of job loss. We rarely see accounting and finance job loss in SMBs because of implementation of a new system. Personnel are simply put to work performing different, more productive work. However, the structure of IT departments is highly subject to change. The programmer who has supported the old green-screen system for twenty years has a difficult choice of upgrading their skills or changing jobs. Hopefully, SMB owners and managers deal with this situation with consideration and foresight.

X. Other Assessments to Make

In this chapter you'll learn:
- *Situations when key company projects clash for resources*

In addition to assessing your personnel for project management and participation on the implementation team, there are a number of other factors to assess in your overall company to determine if timing and resources are appropriate to support a major project.

Case Study: A Rapid Implementation Completed within Two Weeks

By December 1992, my company had grown to five people. One of my employees brought several prospects with him after his previous employer had gone bankrupt. In very short succession, we had three implementations.

A manufacturing company wanted the best of all factors: fast, low cost, and full functionality. We started planning this one two months in advance when the client made the decision to migrate to the new system over the holiday season. Autumn was always their busiest season and then the entire company closed for two weeks over the holidays. In 1992, the management team cancelled the vacation for the administrative and accounting personnel, paid them for the time, and mandated they would work the two weeks to implement Great Plains.

One technician completed the migration of data while another implementer finished training. The small, close-knit staff of ten always cross trained so they spent the first week in training classes – not my usual recommendation. Forty hours of training is usually brutal; these folks, all minority owners, were lively and engaging, keeping up the pace of the classes.

Then they went to work and cut over to the migrated data. They spent a week with two sets of data: one was prototype, one was live. They pounded data and transactions through the prototype, discovering issues and testing changes. On the last day of work, they went live.

This client left some loose ends with their migration. There are modules and functions we can easily defer in a rapid implementation.

Bank Reconciliation is a much easier implementation when completed after a month of system use. You won't have to input nearly as many outstanding checks and deposits derived from the legacy system. If your company is large or has financial management at its heart with multiple checking accounts, this method likely isn't feasible for you.

Financial Statements can be completed after the Go Live. Typically, the Go Live is a month end (not required, but common), so the first financial statements from the new system aren't due until sometime in the month after implementation. An SMB company can easily survive for several months with simple financial statements.

Treat the GL (General ledger) like the bucket it is. Although the distribution from every transaction ends up in the GL, in a small company little day-to-day transactional work is done in the GL. Initially, the chart of accounts must be designed before other modules are implemented, but once that input is finished you can defer GL training a few weeks.

The implementation was on time and on budget. Aside from assessing individual personnel on the implementation team, the company had evaluated the time of year and the seasonality of their sales then picked a successful (for them) January first Go Live date.

This successful implementations defied another common project management challenge: drop dead dates are usually disastrous for implementations. Using the project management technique, "Agile," their goals for their implementation time period and functionality were flexible. Their key goal to implement by January first made other goals fluid. In this particular case, they gave up little and still met their Go Live goal.

Case Study: Challenged Company

Challenged Company did everything right, in my opinion, during their selection process. They narrowed their initial choices down to two competitive software products. Because of strategic criteria—see the chapter on software selection—they eliminated one product early in their process so they found a third product to evaluate so they felt they had two good choices. I still won the deal because of my prior business relationship with the manufacturing manager.

We seemed to be off to a good start until I started having problems getting in contact with the CFO. I waved the red flag after a week and was advised the CFO was no longer the project manager. She had the annual audit to which she had to devote her time. Project management was delegated to a competent employee, who was very organized and communicative, but he had a full time job before the implementation, and the company had no one to backfill his position. In addition, he had never been a project manager.

Even though the CFO was no longer the project manager, all major decisions still had to be approved by her. The new project manager was committed to a forty-hour week and nothing more. The project slowed down. Then we regained the CFO's attention, pushed the Go Live date out a month, and things moved forward.

Then another break in communication occurred for two weeks. This time I rerouted a plane trip to drop in on my client in Santa Fe. The CFO had been temporarily relocated to an international satellite office which was having inventory problems due to the termination of that location's manager.

Opportunities and challenges don't usually schedule themselves to our client's advantage, but this client would have had a more successful project had more weight been given to the needs of the implementation project.

While this project was challenged, it was eventually completed successfully because the company ownership and the CFO willingly pushed the Go Live date out. However, the company continued to have configuration and training issues for nearly a year. I made five trips to Santa Fe that year.

XI. Enabling Rapid or Low-cost Implementation Through Prioritization

In this chapter you'll learn:
- *Setup options that must come first and are hard to change later*
- *What functions and modules can be considered for later implementation*

Managers in SMB companies more stringently prioritize their resources and make sacrifices than managers in large companies. I've never met an entrepreneur or SMB manager who isn't constantly overwhelmed, making choices as to what needs attention first and what won't get their attention. When you deploy rapidly, the trick is to maintain control over what you defer and when you regain it.

Within Dynamics GP there are several options which are very difficult to undo or change after the system has been put into operation:

Account Framework Can't Be Deferred

The Account Framework is defined when Dynamics GP is first installed. Code is installed on the server then GP Utilities is started. The Account Framework is input within GP Utilities and is the umbrella under which all company Account Formats must fit. There is a third-party product that enables change of the Account Framework, but the best situation is to define it adequately in the first place. Too small and you may not have the flexibility you need as you grow.

Fiscal Year Setup Shouldn't be Deferred

Fiscal Year set up is another important set up option that's difficult to change after posting of transactions in the system. Changing it requires use of SQL scripting, reconciling utilities, and indexing utilities.

General Ledger Reporting Ledger Setup

Deactivating Reporting Ledgers can't be changed through typical set up options, so mark this correctly the first time.

Inventory Sites Linked to General Ledger Account Segment

Once inventory sites have been linked to sites, only a SQL script can undo the link.

Creating Customer or Vendor Master Records without Classes

This set up option isn't a major mess, just an unfortunate loss of functionality. Vendor and Customer Classes facilitate set up and change of the master records. Except with a SQL Script, there isn't an easy way to insert classes after the master records are created.

Case Study: A Low-cost Implementation Completed with Twenty Service Hours

- The client's success was primarily based on the fact that he had been using Great Plains Accounting (GPA) on DOS for many years. He asked and we confirmed: much of the process flow in Dynamics GP was similar to GPA.

- With his IT staff, he updated his GPA with the latest available service pack and stabilized it there for the prototype term—approximately six months.
- I would rate him as being above the average Dynamics GP user's technical skillset.
- His use of GPA and Dynamics GP was limited to the financial modules:
  - General Ledger
  - Payables
  - Receivables
  - Bank Reconciliation
  - Fixed Assets
- He and his internal IT staff installed the software on a single desktop computer.
- He migrated a copy of GPA to Dynamics GP using the technical migration manual in order to create a prototype on which to train.
- He scheduled himself and his staff for the free, online training webinars available through the Microsoft CustomerSource web site.
- He maintained training skills through daily use of Dynamics GP throughout the prototype period.
- He has always maintained the software maintenance plan for GPA and then Dynamics GP because he obtains most of his own support through CustomerSource.
- This user didn't have a deadline to meet; he wanted to migrate the live company when he was confidently ready.
- Shortly before the live migration, he met with us. He had accumulated all the questions for one meeting.
- Out of that meeting, he scheduled us for a variety of tasks he felt were best completed by us.
- We used about ten hours for document formatting.
- We used the other ten hours for financial statement formatting, doing much of the work while training him.

Defer Implementation of Some Modules or Functionality

The most common module we see deferred is Fixed Assets. That's a very practical decision unless your company's primary focus deals with fixed assets. I have one client I implemented in 1999 that decided the last module they would implement would be Fixed Assets. The project was scheduled and deferred every year until 2006 when it was finally completed.

Human Resources is another frequently-deferred module.

You may implement Receivables for your Go Live, but defer Customer/Vendor Consolidations, National Accounts, or Returns Management into the second or third month of operations.

Training that can be Deferred

See Chapter 15 for a thorough discussion about training tactics. Review the tactics that facilitate a rapid Go Live:

- Conduct training for groups of employees appropriate for their jobs. Not everyone needs to review set up options.
- Postpone yearend routines training, but insure you schedule it prior to yearend.

A Well-funded Project in a Large Company

System selection in many SMB companies goes like this: The champion, the person who wants a new system the most, jumps to step ten to look at demonstrations with three to seven resellers. The champion picks one system to show to the final decision maker, step twelve; hopefully, step sixteen is undertaken; then they skip to step eighteen. Experienced project managers and implementers insure you won't lose the functionality permanently or have an expensive remodeling process.

A well-funded larger company will go through these types of phases. This list is not all inclusive:

1. Formation of a selection committee
2. Engagement of an internal project manager to lead that committee
3. Development of goals and objectives
4. Development of a needs analysis
5. A business process redesign may be undertaken and documented
6. The needs analysis is refined and issued
7. An RFP (Request for Proposal) will be generated
8. An assessment of the RFP reduces the list of possibilities
9. An RFQ (Request for Quote) will be generated
10. Extensive conference room demonstrations will be undertaken
11. The list of software developers and resellers is further reduced
12. More extensive prototypes and demonstrations are prepared
13. A final solution is selected
14. The final vendor and client complete a business process analysis related expressly to the selected software
15. A fit-gap analysis is prepared
16. System set up options, customizations, and reports are designed
17. The prototype is implemented
18. Customizations and reports are developed inside of the prototype
19. The prototype is extensively tested
20. The project plan and budget are refined and change orders are common
21. Training for and deployment of the live system commences
22. The system goes live
23. System operations are surveyed and compared against goals and objectives
24. Outstanding issues are resolved
25. The customer issues a statement of satisfaction and the system and personnel move into a support stage

For a large company, this is absolutely the right extent of methodology to use to implement a business management system. Processes are complex and span multiple departments and hundreds if not thousands of personnel. Communication requires a great deal more work than in a SMB company.

Case Study: High Growth Company

One of my client company former presidents was very good at programming and marketing in addition to his entrepreneurial skills of managing the company. Along with a new product developed by another owner in 1998, he devised a breakthrough marketing strategy that kicked off an uncontrollable growth spurt. Like all entrepreneurs managing rapid growth, he had to make choices where to spend his time and money. He determined he could no longer maintain the custom accounting and project management system he had personally written so he transitioned the accounting to QuickBooks with the plan to continue to integrate his project management software. He quickly realized he'd made a bad decision.

His custom program integrated poorly to QuickBooks. The entrepreneur's programming skill set and the language which he had used were obsolete; he couldn't find anyone to take his place as a programmer to fix the integration. QuickBooks was overwhelmed with the transaction entry volume and became unstable when only partially through the first year of use. The financial reporting and business intelligence tools to manage cash, assets, and payables weren't available.

I was referred to the entrepreneur, not knowing that several other consultants in his area had already attempted to work with him and had given up. All entrepreneurs are strong willed about their business. I can make that unsubstantiated statement as well as I can say the sun will always rise until the end of time. Weak willed entrepreneurs aren't entrepreneurs for very long. It's just a matter of finding out what they hold their opinions about.

As I started to pull components together for him and complete my process analysis, I found he was strong willed about keeping his administration processes simple. I knew I could put together the right set of integrated products for him, but I was concerned whether he would listen to me long enough for us to get a successful ending.

While the business system need was obvious, the bigger need was timekeeping. The company needed to reduce the losses from projects going over budget because the timekeeping system didn't feed well into the project management system. The entrepreneur knew this was his biggest problem, but he also knew he had to implement the core general ledger, payables, and receivables first.

He and I knew the core of the apple came first. I didn't want him picking a poison apple though, a core business system that wasn't a good choice, even if that was my product. I thought he was rushing into selection of the core modules too fast and, at this point, I wasn't even charging for my time. He was rushing because he wanted his new business system in place by January first.

Because of his programming skills, he thought he could overcome any slight mismatch between time management, project accounting, and his core modules with integration routines and programs. As a system analyst and implementation master, I know that integration is one of the weakest points in a business system.

We had a great meeting and he slowed his selection process down. We talked about integration failures and successes; how he could pick three great products, but if they didn't integrate well, he'd have another failure. We were in agreement with process, integration, and implementation order.

We didn't agree on payroll; I said, "Outsource because I thought his staff was weak on reporting payroll taxes."

He said, "Too expensive."

This entrepreneur's staff stabilized on the financial modules then implemented a time management system (not the one I initially recommended, but they selected one that works for them); after a year, they started customizing project reports. They switched to outsourced payroll about two years after the Go Live.

Multiple staff changes have been made without anyone losing their job. They've hired and inserted personnel between the entrepreneur and the first bookkeeper with whom I worked. Revenue growth continued for a number of years at an uncontrollable rate.

This implementation was a success; the company became wildly successful. I would implement different third-party products, and I wouldn't have invested resources in payroll, so I think their systems would have gotten to a better state faster. But I'm the reseller looking back, not the person who dealt with all the other issues that undoubtedly occurred.

Fluid Goals—the Agile Approach

When you compress your implementation timeframe, training then implementation of each module occurs in close sequence. Here are some tactics to consider for re-prioritization inside of a rapid, agile implementation.

Financial statement formatting isn't a critical Go Live function. Financial statements need posted information in the general ledger before they are useful. Obtain the training; then design and format your initial financial statements after Go Live. Usually you need the first financial statements from the new system thirty to forty-five days after Go Live.

Bank reconciliation usually occurs at least a month after Go Live. Defer its training and implementation until the third or fourth week after Go Live.

Input your payables in your legacy system, print the checks, and hold them for up to a month. Auditors and CPA's stop quivering. These are small, unaudited companies I'm writing about.

Nearly everyone can defer doctor and dentist appointments, miss a ball game, or put off a long weekend with the relatives inside of a rapid implementation. But be careful. When your implementation stretches out past its schedule (whatever the timeframe), life happens; employees lose flexibility with deferring all their other things in life and their normal work load. Once an implementation goes over its schedule, the schedule usually continues to stretch out. With every week that passes the chance of failure increases.

XII. Count Your Eggs Before They Hatch

What you'll learn in this chapter:
- *Why I consider a prototype vital to success*
- *Tips and stages of a prototype*

You're ready to plan the conditions for your prototype. You may plan it with a consultant or decide you can do it on your own. You might use a free thirty-day hosted version or need to have a private cloud environment configured for you. If you're planning to purchase perpetual licenses, you might prototype on your reseller's not-for-resale version of the software (and their hardware—that's vital to licensing rights) to avoid the substantial outlay of cash for the software until you're absolutely certain you've picked the best software for your company.

You may outright purchase the software especially if a significant time sensitive discount was offered. For the prototype, you likely need fewer licenses than once the system is live. On the other hand, you may have obtained financing for the hardware, software, support plan, and consulting services. Financing may necessitate purchase of the full system up front.

We have found the prototype to be the best tool for determining the software fit, the extent of customization required, and the most accurate estimate of the personnel and financial resources required to complete the implementation.

A prototype lowers your risk and may do so prior to your expenditure of nonrefundable costs for software and the majority of services. The prototype provides the optimum environment for design and testing because of the limited quantity of data.

We've prototyped in as little as two days. Also, we've taken the prototype directly into the live system. The typical midsize firm will take two to eight weeks to prototype. Work with your reseller to document how much of your data will be used and what your specific goals are.

At the conclusion of the prototype, when you've been assisted by a reseller or consultant, you should have the relevant components of:

- An updated software quotation
- The best estimate of the time required for extraction and cleanup of legacy data
- The best estimate of time required for installation, training, implementation, and customization
- A specification list of replacement and upgraded hardware
- A project plan listing the steps of implementation, scheduled training classes, milestones for implementation, and cutover dates
- If you're using a reseller or consultant, an engagement letter with terms upon which you've both agreed (if you're working closely with them at the start of the prototype, that should already be in place)

The prototype better identifies the scope of the implementation. Company management can better plan for and obtain the financial resources that will be necessary. Prototypes help lower the overall risk associated with business solution implementations.

Owners of small companies who think they can't afford a prototype are the very owners who must have a prototype. They have no room for risk.

If the consultant has implemented six other similar companies and you verified that by talking to at least two of them, your prototype might be simple but it absolutely should not be skipped. It's still necessary to assist your consultant with assessing the unique combination of your personnel, the software, and your data.

Timing of a Prototype

SMBs should complete a prototype because if they don't they will likely run out of flexibility to adequately budget and plan for resources for the implementation. I observed a competitor completing such an expensive prototype of a system, once the company paid the $70,000 for the prototype, they realized they couldn't afford to implement even though they determined they had picked a good software match for their needs. They eventually implemented four years later.

Midmarket companies purchasing perpetual licenses should prototype just prior to buying the software or just after buying a portion of the software user licenses, depending upon the reseller's license agreement with the software developer. When we're in complete control of the prototype in our environment and plan a rapid "conference room" prototype with an extremely small set of data inside of two weeks, we'll frequently prototype for the client with our software license.

If your situation involves complex, unique hardware and software combinations, you may need to purchase most of your licenses and hardware in which to prototype. Government agencies, quasigovernment agencies, and not-for-profit agencies have unique budget environments that require comprehensive prototyping. It's unlikely these entities will ever implement rapidly. It's typical for them to obtain funding for up to multiple stages:

- Assessment of the current situation
- Preparation of a needs analysis
- Preparation of a request for quote
- Assessment of the quotations
- Preparation of a prototype
- Once the prototype identifies the total budget, obtain funding for the final project
- The final project
- Plus an extraordinary number of change orders for anything out of scope

What's Involved in a Prototype

Everything that will be utilized in your final implementation should be considered for a prototype. Think of a prototype as your insurance policy. Insurance companies issuing policies assess your risk factors and base their premium on those factors calculated against the volume of your business revenue. If your business involves nuclear reactors, aviation control, power generation facilities, medical equipment, financial investment processes, etc., your prototype will be a Performance Simulation.

In the 1980's, my neighbor of eight years was a visionary. He held multiple degrees in physics and engineering, had obtained several patents, started and sold a company, taught at local universities, and (when I last visited him several years after he had moved) become a merger/acquisition specialist for one of the international CPA organizations . He advised me once if I called a prototype a prototype, I could charge $100 per hour. If I called it a "Preoperational Performance Simulation," I could charge $400 per hour.

The Starting Point of a Prototype

The prototype starts with the output from the system: management reports, financial reports, checks, invoices, and purchase orders, for example. Only what goes into the system can come out in the form of information and reports so you must start with the output to determine the input.

A prototype with a limited set of data helps you cycle through the implementation process and refine the design. In a rapid implementation, we start with one year of historical data from the general ledger or one historical year of ending balances. That insures that we can create the financial statements in an acceptable format and proves that we balance to the historical year. If we've made the effort to extract historical general ledger entries for the prototype, we'll usually be able to retain that data for the live system.

Legacy Data

The ease of extraction of legacy data depends on how old the system is, whether someone who knows the old database is still available, and what condition the data is in. If you're determined to implement with detailed legacy data, extraction must be prototyped in all cases. Difficulties with legacy data can stall or even halt an implementation; therefore, extraction, cleaning, and loading of legacy data must always be prototyped.

Read much more information about legacy data throughout the book and especially in Chapters XV, XVII, and XVIII.

Third-party Software

If you're considering the use of third-party software, you must test the integration during the prototype. Integration is the Achilles heel of business management systems.

So many methods of integration can be used, it's worthwhile to develop an understanding of the methods and pound on them during the prototype. Like buying a used car evaluated before purchase by a trusted mechanic, have an integration method assessed by a good software integration specialist if it isn't explained or working to your satisfaction.

Case Study: Custom Software

One of our clients is still recovering from a botched implementation ten years ago. A novice reseller sold them on the need for a custom point of sale system for their industry. In an effort to keep costs down, the planning, prototyping, integration, and testing were minimized or eliminated. The implementation was financed and initiated during the company's slack season. A rapid implementation was underway without identifying it was rapid. The busy season for this client started with a rush on the first warm weekend in spring.

The consulting organization failed to plan and monitor the project; the programmer failed to accurately estimate the customization development hours and ultimately used all the service funds, leaving nothing for training and support. The implementation encroached on the busy season, causing the employees to implement on their own with unpaid overtime hours, making what I call uninformed decisions.

Prototype Custom Software

Custom software development can be so complex, it's a book topic all by itself covered in multiple books—search for "software development project management" on the internet to find over 1,600 titles.

The development project should be organized into several phases and closely monitored by a project manager. The first phase should always be a design phase resulting in written specifications, budget and timeframe. The software should be developed and heavily tested within the prototype.

Documentation is frequently omitted in many customization projects; documentation should include both technical specifications and user manuals. I consider it a grave mistake to omit documentation. Programmers and employees come and go. Without documentation you could be in a very expensive situation requiring rewrite of the software, or at the very least, paying a new developer to come up to speed on the software to support you.

In addition the code should be placed in escrow with full revelation to you of all passwords should the developer go out of business or, as we like to say, "Got hit by the beer truck." Unless your contract with the developer specifically deals with ownership the developer owns the code as a copyrighted work. You may think you own the code because you paid for the development, but it's intellectual property covered by unique laws. Consult an attorney in your state for assistance.

If you're planning on a customization, you're likely not doing a rapid implementation, at least not during the customization development phase.

Prototype Reports

If you have key reports that will impact your business, the production of those reports must be included in the prototype. Default reports existing in the standard software may suffice; default reports may be slightly modified; custom reports may be required. Failure to incorporate report design in the prototype is a significant cause of underestimating the scope of an implementation.

Prototype Cost

Your prototype may use from fifteen to sixty percent of your total consulting budget. A prototype lowers your risk and may do so prior to your expenditure of nonrefundable costs for software and the majority of services. The prototype provides the optimum environment for design and testing because of the limited quantity of data; therefore, analysis of the prototype process reveals that it lowers the overall cost of implementation.

Results and Benefits of the Prototype

- A demonstration of the software with your data
- The design of any customizations
- Proven integration of third-party products
- Design of custom reports
- Proof of implementation on your hardware or a simulation of your hardware
- A more accurate, complete software quotation
- A more accurate estimate of the consulting time required for installation, training, implementation, and customization
- A detailed project plan
- An engagement letter with the terms upon which you've both agreed
- Diminished number of Change Orders for additional services
- Training with familiar data

XIII. Needs Analysis

What you'll learn in this chapter:
- *Methods for a rapid needs analysis*
- *Situations where a needs analysis may not be needed*

I have participated in numerous implementations which follow a needs analysis completed by consultants following lean practices who analyze, diagnose, design, and test in great detail. Other requirement analyses stand out in my mind like a $30,000 needs analysis completed by the local office of a worldwide consulting group for a private company. For any company with the straightforward financial accounting needs, a CPA with one of larger firms in town could have recommended a good product with one phone call.

Case Study: Not-for-profit Recommendation

I was once contacted to contribute my time as a favor to an IT consultant who was donating his time to a large Pacific Northwest not-for-profit entity. The CFO was late for the meeting, but he finally stormed into the room very angry about an estimate for a needs analysis which he had just received, "For a whole lot less than $45,000, someone should be able to tell me three software systems that we should consider. I can put that money to much better use saving lives."

I spoke up and said, "I don't know a whole lot about your company in detail, but I know the industry quite well," and I cited the three products a large not-for-profit should evaluate. My product, while heavily used in not-for-profit companies, was the smallest and least expensive. I advised him of the approximate cost, features, benefits, and weaknesses of each. Being quite gracious, he thanked me for saving him a bunch of money in less than five minutes. Ultimately he evaluated the top two products and deployed within the next six months.

Who Needs a Detailed Needs Analysis

Public agencies, public companies or large private firms may benefit from detailed needs assessment projects, or they may be required to complete them. SMB owners usually prioritize differently where they spend their time and money. They take broader strokes in the initial rapid stages of growth to maximize sales, minimize expenses, and make the best use their assets and cash resources.

The first system implemented by most small company owners is probably an entry level system without a lot of options to analyze and modify. Needs analyses weren't typically prepared. The small company deploys around the system as the system exists. Growth and complexity occurs; the company needs to move up into a midmarket business management system.

The issue that I see, analyzing and duplicating current workflow and process may not help a small company make the leap that it needs. It may be better for the small company to transition the simple system as rapidly as possible into industry-standard workflow and processes with a midmarket product that's flexible and can be modified after the personnel have accustomed themselves to the new system.

This concept works well with a system like Dynamics GP. With Dynamics AX and NAV the configuration must be much more closely matched to the company workflow and needs. AX and NAV are less frequently implemented following use of an entry level system; however, transitioning rapidly into these two products is possible if the configuration is closely matched to the client's industry.

Recognize that "rapid" is always a matter of relativity. A typical implementation of Dynamics GP takes two to four months. A typical implementation of NAV is four to twelve months and a typical implementation of AX takes six to twenty-four months.

If you skip the needs analysis, your success will be dependent upon a reseller who has configured for your industry. Approximately sixty percent of my clients are in wholesale distribution because Portland, OR is a major West

Coast port, and Oregon governors have been very active creating trading relationships around the Pacific Rim. I've deployed many implementations of Microsoft Dynamics GP when we didn't complete a lengthy needs analysis. The question is, are these successful deployments? I can confidently say, "Yes."

Case Study: Implementing without an Initial Needs Analysis

An implementation of a company with revenue of $60,000 is a good example of when I skipped an initial detailed needs analysis. I found in initial queries of company personnel they were primarily running the company on Excel worksheets. The legacy system was used after the sales were made, the inventory was physically verified, or the purchase order issued. Every person in the company used a slightly different workflow and process. To have completed an initial detailed needs analysis would have been extremely time consuming when the legacy system was breaking down daily.

In this case, inputting substantial data into a prototype and designing the system around the data flow as it was created in the new system was more useful than performing a needs analysis and creating a workflow based on the current processes. The legacy processes were broken and fragmented; it was a good idea to start over. My team and the CFO prepared a rapid prototype and simply dictated to the various departments what their new workflow was going to be. The implementation and workflow continued to change for the first year; however, every change was prototyped and tested before being deployed in the live company.

Case Study: Midsize Company without a Needs Analysis

Other circumstances may indicate you could combine the needs analysis with the prototype phase. I deployed a client whose personnel had never managed their financial statements, general ledger, payables, receivables, or bank reconciliation. Their parent company managed those modules.

Personnel focused solely on the job cost management of inventory, sales, purchasing, and assets.

I was talking with the president when he received a management report produced from the legacy system. I knew the financial analyst had worked on the report for three days. The president accepted the report and without so much as glancing at the executive summary on the first page, dropped the report into his trash can.

I realized I was working with personnel who could have little idea of what they needed. The long-term employees were entrenched in job costing, not financial management. The prior parent company had designed the legacy business management system using a tier-one enterprise system. The design of that product centered on the parent company's transaction volume to meet their manufacturing needs. The revenue and expense account structure never met my new client's needs which were driven by job costing.

The lack of an internal design to carry forward caused problems during the implementation. Over the first six weeks of design, the new controller had me create three different general ledger charts of accounts. We started with financial statement templates and worked backwards to a chart of accounts in three time-consuming iterations. As our deadline for Go Live approached, the project team knew they had to move forward so they picked one design after an intensive whiteboard session. The accounting manager had an extremely good grasp of job cost requirements which drove the design we selected. She had quite a job eventually translating the entries from the manufacturing chart of accounts into the design the project team had selected.

Two situations assisted us as the project team worked through design. The industry manager from the new parent company was actively engaged during the implementation because of the substantial transition occurring with the ownership of the client. In addition, he managed three similar companies and we were able to meet with one of them. I greatly admire that manager for allowing the project team to develop its own design rather than forcing a design on them.

My client is a holding company with multiple subsidiary companies, multiple physical locations of assets and operations, jobs spread across the physical locations, sensitive intercompany transactions, and international reporting requirements. The company is operating well with the design selected and additional new modules have been deployed as the company grows. The accounting manager has utilized the job costing module to meet numerous different needs within the company

Tip	Comment on the Tip
Find out what similar companies are using.	My client had a clear advantage with a sister company owned by their new parent.
Work backwards from your financial statements and management reports.	The system reports only what is input, so working backwards from the reports identifies the segment structure, data fields, and core design of the chart of accounts. Look at the master records first: • Chart of accounts • Customer records • Vendor records • Inventory records • Job records • Employee records
When a legacy system isn't worth mapping and you have little time, gather everyone's reports.	Reports provide you with the data fields you need to incorporate into your design. I utilize a very simple questionnaire that I keep with a copy of each report sample. I don't get copies of 200-page reports. I take the first page, one in the middle, and the last page. Then I find out who prepares the report, who receives the report, and from where the data is retrieved. On a scale of one to ten, I have everyone rate the priority of the report. When I point out to everyone that every report is rated a ten, we reprioritize the reports.

Don't omit electronic "reports."	These are the executive dashboards, information transmitted by email, and (heaven forbid) handwritten reports.
I insure I understand how the report is used, how often it's produced, and the date range of the information.	I go through each report and add a sheet listing all the data points on the reports. Then I spread it out on the living room floor and group the reports by the common data points.
I correlate the legacy reports and data points with current reports in Dynamics GP.	Then the project team and I can review the reports, prioritize whether they want to accept the current reports or customize reports. This type of rapid needs analysis takes two to three days instead of several weeks or months.
Be willing to accept new formats.	I've found that some users can be extremely set in their ways about report format. If you want to deploy rapidly and without expensive report customizations, insure your users are willing to accept new formats.
Most companies pay bills the same way.	There are variations; electronic transmission versus checks being the biggest issue. Usually your payables cycle is the least important. Rely on industry-standard methods and push payables design to the end.
Unless you are a payroll processing company, outsource payroll.	SMBs can't typically afford a payroll specialist and one bad fumble paying or reporting payroll taxes could cost a lot
Concentrate on your revenue stream.	Take a close look at every segment of data you track regarding your customers, their transactions, and your inventory. If you get this cycle right, you've got eighty percent of the design.
Deploy Without Historical Data	We tackle this issue with every implementation. See Chapter XIX for alternatives.

Integrate historical data after the rapid implementation of only the functionality needed for current operations.	We've integrated historical data after the Go Live several times. The challenge is always to keep the control accounts in balance. Invariably transaction dates get muddled.
If you're going to integrate historical data after the Go Live, capture a copy of the data set that balances open receivables, payables, and inventory to the general ledger.	Then you can isolate new entries that may cause the system to get out of balance. In Dynamics GP, routines using Microsoft Excel assist with reconciling subsidiary ledgers to the general ledger control accounts.
Insure all employees start using the new system.	I've experienced multiple instances when an employee struggled so much with the new system, they revert to using the new system thinking they'll catch up with reentry soon. In one case, the employee's action caused failure of the implementation.
With tools to make master record changes, realize your first design doesn't have to be perfect.	With the RMT (Rapid Migration Tool), you can move your data from QuickBooks or Peachtree in a matter of hours. Once the data is in Dynamics GP, use PSTL (Professional Services Tools Library) to convert to a new chart of accounts and more usable customer, vendor, and inventory ID's.

Case Study: Handwritten Reports

I was under fire for six months at one implementation because I had missed the president's key report, but no one could produce a copy. Finally he came back from his vacation home with a copy of a handwritten report on yellow notepaper. I had thrown the originals of those reports away thinking they were useless old notes; they didn't make sense to me. He considered them vital. When I showed him the system-generated reports with the same information, as far as he was concerned, it simply wasn't the same information.

XIV. Rapid Process Workflow Inside the Prototype

What you'll learn in this chapter:
- *What you gain or give up when bypassing the documented process workflow*
- *How a hosted site can help you prototype and document process workflow at low cost*

The initial detailed needs analysis and documented process workflow go hand in hand. If you're bypassing the detailed needs analysis, you're likely bypassing the detailed process workflow.

One of the techniques I've used over the years with many SMB companies is to document the process workflow after completion of the prototype. Quite frankly, the funds for documentation may not exist in an SMB. While I consider this a grave mistake, I've implemented too many small companies seeking to cut initial costs so much that to deny that decision is ever made is akin to sticking my head in a sack. They simply won't pay to document their processes, and I've found it's an equally bad decision for me to work for free. We just work it out in the prototype and keep moving through the implementation. In the larger firms, we:

1. Analyze the entire operation
2. Diagnose problems
3. Draw workflow in Microsoft Visio, document it, and review it with the client
4. Complete our scripting and programming
5. Test the design in the prototype
6. Iterate through Visio, programming, documentation, and review
7. Training and implementation
8. Review, make minor changes, and support

In an SMB, we're quite likely to group steps one to five into a very rapid prototype design. Especially if you've been using an entry-level system, you may want to so substantially change workflow, it's not relevant to document your existing workflow before the transition from your old system. I'm an advocate of the KISS method. Diagram your workflow on a whiteboard and use your Smartphone to take a picture for documentation

Large companies with SOX, HIPAA, etc., guidelines and requirements have no choice but to document processes and procedures and meet extensive change management requirements. Small companies just need to get the job done, ensuring the new system meets their needs.

On www.rapidimplementation.com I've placed a chapter from our internal process workflow document. I use the Windows Snipping Tool to take screen shots, pasting them into Paint to add red circles or highlights; then I paste them into my Word document.

One of my SQL engineers nearly fainted once when I showed him how to "correct" a document he had printed to PDF. The transaction was correct within Dynamics GP, but the engineer hadn't correctly set up the contract and project so the change order wouldn't calculate cost correctly. I viewed it on screen, snipped it, pasted it into Paint, made the change, pasted the graphic into Word, and saved it as a PDF document type. It's not a process that would pass an audit, but it demonstrates that you don't need complex and expensive publishing programs to produce a process workflow document.

If you have to limit your investment of time and money in an implementation project in order to implement it quickly, condense the first phases into the prototype. Use the prototype to push and test transactions to determine whether the system meets all your detailed needs. Once any configuration changes and customizations are made, use the prototype to document your process workflow.

Frequently you uncover more with the prototype than you find with the detailed needs analysis. I assisted a tribal government with business process analysis. They had a fixed budget and tight timeline for the needs analysis, having previously received the recommendation from their CPA's to purchase either Dynamics GP or Dynamics SL and implement by the end of the calendar year. Their electronic banking needs were demanding; Dynamics GP was the better fit.

However, we didn't dive deep enough into definition of Payables ACH functionality in the needs analysis. They had one payment out of over 400 that needed to be transmitted to a small Canadian bank. At that time, Dynamics GP didn't meet that minor detailed requirement. We uncovered that detail in the prototype stage and developed the workaround—they called the transaction to the bank for the ACH payment for that one transaction.

One of the newest and cheapest methods to complete a prototype is to locate one of the thirty-days-free Dynamics GP hosting sites. These sites are Public Deployments (see Chapter VI), so you may be restricted by requirements on what data you can input, but they certainly help you start at low cost.

The danger with these sites, if you start with no training, you're most likely to get confused and give up. A monthly charge for a few users is certainly worth the access you'll gain to online training webinars.

XV. The Right Tools

What you'll learn in this chapter:
- *Tools for use for a rapid implementation*
- *A summary of Microsoft Dynamics® GP tools*

A Little History First

While I've frequently mentioned Dynamics GP in prior chapters, this chapter is exclusively about technical tools for Dynamics GP so I'll provide some history of the product.

What is now known as Microsoft Dynamics GP was formerly known as Microsoft Great Plains, which was formerly Dynamics, Dynamics CS+, and eEnterprise—depending upon the underlying database. Those three products started out as Great Plains Dynamics.

The first true Windows business management software, Dynamics GP was introduced to the market in March 1993. Throughout the remainder of the 1990's the product was available on three databases: C-tree, Btrieve, and Microsoft SQL. During the years roughly from 1998 to 2002, Great Plains Software and then Microsoft discontinued the product on C-tree and Btrieve.

Many software tools are available for Microsoft Dynamics® AX, GP, NAV, and SL. My team is most familiar with GP, and its tools are the most complete set because it's the oldest business management product based on Microsoft SQL. Industry-standard software programs are like people in that regard; as we get older, we acquire more nice stuff.

That may leave you wondering though about how old GP is and, therefore, how long is it going to be around. We frequently face competitors who create doubt about GP's longevity, yet business management product roadmaps are projected out by Microsoft for longer than any competitor's product. That roadmap exists for the Dynamics GP product as well as for AX and NAV.

Microsoft's policy to roll license revenue between its Dynamics products ensures an even sounder investment in its Dynamics products.

Case Study: RapidStart Migration

A recent implementation of ours used the Rapid Migration tool to move data from QuickBooks to Dynamics GP 2010. The implementation started with a prototype so the client could test various set up options. Their initial goal was to minimize service costs, and we agreed to a shoestring budget of 100 hours, clearly specifying the work that they had to complete and the work that we would complete.

The client wanted to do primary design, training, and project management internally to keep consulting costs down. Personnel spoke English, German, French, and Italian; making decisions was a time consuming process and they didn't want to pay us to wait for all the translation time.

The client started with the concept that all their companies would be included within one database. Eventually they decided to break apart the one database into multiple company databases because they wanted tighter security restrictions.

We used the Rapid Migration tool for data export from QuickBooks. Then we used more tools to make changes to master records and to import historical general ledger transactions in their prototype. The Rapid Configuration tool eventually pushed the configuration from the first company into the other five companies.

What follows is a discussion of the various tools we used.

RapidStart for Microsoft Dynamics® GP

For later versions of Dynamics GP (9.0 and later), two primary tools for rapid implementation were developed: Rapid Migration and Rapid

Configuration. Those tools are now bundled in a product called RapidStart for Microsoft Dynamics® GP released in January 2013. The RapidStart tools run as services and include the following:

- RapidStart Services Plug-in for Microsoft Office which helps edit data
- RapidStart Configuration which enables the configuration and import of basic setup information into Dynamics GP
- RapidStart Migration which allows the export of basic setup information from QuickBooks or Peachtree and the subsequent import of that data into Dynamics GP.

RapidStart is free once you're a licensed user of Dynamics and are available whether software is perpetually licensed or is subscription licensed on a hosted network. The tools are easily utilized by an experienced GP consultant or internal technical personnel after a little practice. The first version of the tools were wizard driven. The RapidStart tools released in January 2013 have changed to a questionnaire-based user interface.

RapidStart tools assist you with exporting, cleaning, and importing master records, subsidiary module open transactions, and general ledger beginning balance transactions. Technically, this process is referred to as ECL (Extract, Clean, and Load). The tools can also create Excel worksheets within which you can modify the data before integrating it. RapidStart handles these records:

- General ledger chart of accounts and beginning balances in an un-posted work batch
- Customer master records and open transactions in an un-posted work batch
- Vendor master records and open transactions in an un-posted work batch
- Open Sales Quotes, Orders, Invoices, and Back Orders
- Open Purchase Orders
- Item master records
- Employee master records

RapidStart Migration

The RapidStart Migration tool extracts Intuit QuickBooks or Sage Peachtree data for import into a Dynamics GP company database. Before data is migrated the user manuals assist with preparation processes in Dynamics GP and QuickBooks or Peachtree.

RapidStart Configuration

This tool can be used three different ways:
1. An industry-standard template configuration can be created in Dynamics then imported into a new Dynamics company database.
2. An industry-standard configuration can be prepared in an Excel template then imported into a new Dynamics company database. The tool can also be used to modify the configuration.
3. An existing Dynamics GP company's setup information can be used as a template to setup additional companies.

We have many multi-location or multi-corporation clients using the Configuration Tool with as many as ninety company databases (the last time we checked). This tool is invaluable for clients we call "serial entrepreneurs" or holding companies.

Computeration Zap!

Within QuickBooks and Peachtree, several clients were using simple job cost functionality which equated to Dynamics GP's Analytical Accounting dimensions. The RapidStart tool doesn't integrate with Analytical Accounting so we use a custom product, Computeration's "Zap! Integration," to fill the integration gap. Zap uses the eConnect module and provides friendly error messages to advise when something doesn't integrate. It also tracks those errors and allows for easy re-integration once the error is corrected.

Zap is a suite of integration enhancement modules for Dynamics GP developed by Computeration. Initially custom developed to simplify an integration routine for a client, we added onto the tool and starting providing it to the open Dynamics GP market. With this specialized integration tool, you can quickly transfer your data from Excel spreadsheets into your General Ledger, Payables, Receivables, Purchase Orders, or Sales Order Processing with a single click. Zap you're done.

Zap relies upon the Dynamics GP eConnect module to provide a "hot" integration—that means it's live 24 hours a day. Zap requires about 2 hours of customization for each installation because it has to be uniquely configured on your network. A directory is created for Zap to watch. Drop a correctly configured Excel worksheet into the directory and Zap integrates it, based on the interval you've requested—every minute, every hour, every day, or whenever.

Part of Zap was configured for integration from custom staging databases for insurance, financial, web stores, and retail store integrations. Its user interface tracks the success of the transaction import and provides friendly error messages when transactions don't import. It leaves the incorrect transactions in the Excel file and tells you what needs to be corrected. After you make the corrections, its integration timer imports just the remaining files or you can click a manual reimport button.

Professional Services Tools Library

After a RapidStart migration, a client wanted new general ledger account numbers and customer and vendor ID's. March 1, 2012, Microsoft announced that PSTL (Professional Services Tools Library) would be bundled with the Foundation modules at no charge.

Microsoft personnel call PSTL "pistol;" I call it "postal" but that's what can you expect from a lady with a three-foot-high ceramic chicken in her office.

Included in PSTL among other tools, there are account modifier and combiner tools which translate or merge general ledger account numbers and customer and vendor ID's quickly and accurately.

Reconcile Account Format Utility

After completing a general ledger account change, a good technique is to utilize the reconcile utility at >> Administration landing page >> Utilities >> Reconcile >> Account Format Setup. This will cause the account format to reduce to the desired segment characters.

Follow up with the Setup Checklist

After use of the RapidStart, there is an additional tool internal to Dynamics GP. A Setup Checklist links to every window typically visited during set up. The Setup Checklist is an easy way to track what's in progress and what's been completed. It's best to iterate through this checklist once or twice before using the system to double check all setup options.

Integration Manager

Integration Manager is one of two standard tools to use with Dynamics GP. It has multiple acceptable source table formats. Translation tables can be created to convert accounts and identification codes during the import. VBA (Visual Basic for Applications) scripts can be utilized before, during, and after integration; and can be utilized just once or repetitively. Most transactions are imported into work files giving you the opportunity to review and post the transactions. Transactions for Sales Order processing, Purchase Order Processing, and Bank Reconciliation are imported into open files.

eConnect

eConnect provides access to nearly every Dynamics GP table, accompanied by software rules enabling it to act like a virtual user so characters don't import into date fields, for example. It can be set up with queues; it enables Zap! timed imports.

We've used eConnect to import retail transactions from custom systems and web sites. We've designed a complex staging database that reads customer and sales transactions for an insurance company, importing the customer additions and changes first then going back to get the sales transactions.

eConnect uses .NET technology and generally requires the use of an integration specialist skilled with its use. Many ISVs (Independent Software Vendors) use eConnect with their products.

The following information is quoted from the website for the Microsoft Developer Network:

"eConnect is a collection of tools, components, and interfaces that allow applications to programmatically interact with Microsoft Dynamics GP. The key eConnect components and interfaces include:

A .NET managed code assembly

A Microsoft BizTalk® Application Integration Component (AIC)

Microsoft Message Queuing (MSMQ) services

These eConnect interfaces allow external applications like web storefronts, web services, point-of-sale systems, or legacy applications to integrate with Microsoft Dynamics GP. The external applications can perform actions like creating, updating, retrieving, and deleting back office documents and transactions. While eConnect supplies a large number of documents, not every Microsoft Dynamics GP feature is available through eConnect.

Hint: Throughout the documentation, the terms back office and front office are used. The term back office refers to the financial management system, in this case, Microsoft Dynamics GP. The term front office refers to customer relationship management systems, data warehouses, web sites, or other applications that communicate with the back office.

eConnect allows you to leverage the existing transaction-based business logic of Microsoft Dynamics GP. This allows you to focus your time and energy on creating or enhancing custom applications for the front office." (http://msdn.microsoft.com/en-us/library/aa973831.aspx)

XVI. I'm Taking a Stand: The Egg Came First

What you'll learn in this chapter:
- *Additional information on RapidStart Services for Microsoft Dynamics® GP 2013*

Envision a dinosaur with a few pinfeathers sticking out of it. The kindly Tyrannosaurus Rex mother hops off her nest because her baby has just hatched—a downy chick that represents the new evolution of a T-Rex. That's my basis for maintaining the egg came first.

Microsoft Dynamics® GP 2013 RapidStart Services were hatched fully functional just as this book was preparing to go to publication; just in time for me to do a quick, short chapter on the features and benefits. RapidStart tools are developed for Dynamics AX, GP, and NAV. They have a graphical user interface designed to lead a novice through several steps to assist with a rapid implementation.

For Dynamics GP, you need to begin with a relatively empty new company database containing only a few key setup options; the manual guides you through those requirements. Then you can export data from QuickBooks, Peachtree, or another company database of Dynamics GP, clean the data up in Excel, and continue using the RapidStart tool to import your data into your new company.

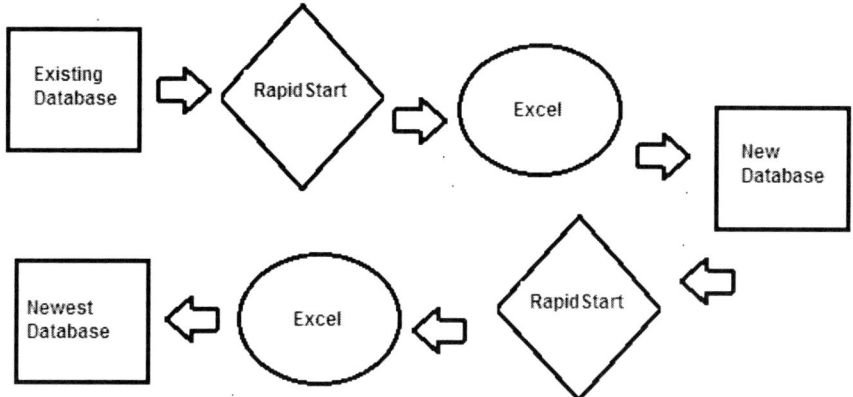

This is obviously helpful when you have five or ten nearly-identical company databases. We have users with 50 or more nearly-identical databases. The driving force for so many databases is the differing ownership which is a common practice with property management firms, serial entrepreneurs, and turnaround specialists who buy properties and companies to either retain them to build their empire or whip them back into shape and resell them at a profit.

In addition, the tool provides obvious help to consultants who specialize in a tight vertical market. They can create a library of templates to use over and over.

New Features in RapidStart for Microsoft Dynamics GP 2013

The Rapid Configuration Tool now layers its methodology into a robust tool for consultants who need to manage multiple projects at any one time. Information from multiple project components flows into the tool and is tracked by the tool without requiring the information to flow in any particular order.

Consultants have the capability to create a library of their projects to return to at any time for future use. Consultants can use a template from the library which may represent up to ninety percent of the configuration work for a company database. Using the interface to Microsoft Excel, the consultant can make changes to the data, save the second template, and push the data into the database for the new client company.

RapidStart 2013 accurately interfaces with new functionality in Dynamics GP 2013 allowing for multiple custom system databases. Companies may have multiple deployments of Dynamics GP in one Microsoft SQL instance; each deployment may have a unique system database where, previously, only one instance of the system database "DYNAMICS" was allowed.

At Computeration, we've deployed Dynamics GP 2013 inside of a virtual environment, layering in the RapidStart Tools and creating our library. We previously had a small library of deployments, but we envision our library will substantially change with this new release.

Of critical importance with any implementation of Dynamics GP, the account framework must be consistent in order to enable attaching the company database to a DYNAMICS system database. While that requirement still stands, the RapidStart Tools with the interim usage of Excel will add one more tool to our workbench to lower implementation costs for SMBs.

XVII. Teaching the Chicks a New Trick

What you'll learn in this chapter:
- *Tips and tricks for effective training*
- *Why certain approaches to training don't work*

High-quality, adequate, and appropriate training is one of the most important investments in your new system that you can make. Therefore, it might end up being one of the highest costs of implementation. It's important to recognize both internal and service provider costs. Generally the more services you obtain from a good trainer, the more effective the training will be. If you complete all your training with internal personnel, expect it to take more time.

I recognize that when your personnel are in training, they aren't doing their other productive work: customer service, sales, production, paying bills, making deposits...so you have a double whammy. You're paying an expensive consultant and probably two to twelve of your employees aren't doing the work that pays for the consultant. That may encourage you to shorten the training.

That's a common but big mistake. Fortunately, business owners frequently recognize their error. Providing additional training is one of the frequent reasons we're called back into an implementation.

Your second plan to keep service provider costs down may be to utilize online training so your personnel can have more flexible hours; work the training into the gaps between their "real work." Online training can work well, but only if you acknowledge the challenge ahead of your personnel and structure the training to accommodate their needs and the reality of the task. An experience I had in school provides a good example.

Case Study: A New System is Like a New Language

I generally consider myself a relatively fast learner, but my methods didn't work with Russian. I started reading War and Peace in sixth grade when the assignment was to produce a book report every month. When I realized I wouldn't finish the book in time to write the review by the due date, I asked my teacher for an extra weekend. He better understood the problem ahead of me and wanted me to develop some understanding of what I was reading; he gave me two additional months to read the book and write the review. I learned to love Russian literature so my efforts grew.

I enrolled in a Russian language class at college, expecting to learn to read Russian literature. I asked my professor in my first class, "How long will it be before I can read War and Peace in Russian?" She laughed and said her advanced students were unable to do so. I was determined to prove her wrong so I spent extra lab time listening to tapes. It was pointless.

The only thing I could remember for more than a day was how to count in Russian. Three hours a week wasn't enough for me to even learn basic words and phrases; I was flunking every written exam. My instructor saw that I was spending extra effort in lab time so she started tutoring me a half hour prior to every test and I was able to respond verbally with high accuracy. This was before the days when I could have required her to provide a verbal exam. I would have received an A. All I earned was simply a "Pass" because of my effort. I can still count in Russian, but I don't remember anything else.

The Russian language and a new business management system require daily immersion to learn them. Fortunately with daily immersion, the new system takes much less time to learn than the Russian language!

Provide for Alternative Learning Styles

My story also illustrates that different students have different learning styles, and the same student with different materials may have different needs. I generally learn by reading, writing, or doing. With Russian, the material needed a different path into a different part of my brain than technical material; for me, verbal training was more effective with a language. Almost all my other classes were technical, mathematical, or theoretical.

Over my career I've found that many people in accounting aren't really accountants. They were at the right place at the right time to get a job. While they range from normal and nice people to truly above average and gifted, they may not have formal education in accounting. They learned their job routines and will learn the new system by repetition of tasks.

You'll find that everyone will have their own methods and tactics to learn. Personally, as a trainer, the ones I dread are the ones that must write everything down instead of reading and annotating the book. If you have a learner like that, expect and plan for slower classes.

The new business management system takes lots of practice to learn. It's not a task to work in between "real work." The only successful way to make the training stick is to allocate uninterrupted time for webinars and practice immediately prior to your employees using the system. With my most successful implementations, I train the designers early in the project and immediately schedule them to use the system at least an hour a day up to implementation. Just prior to implementation, the company designers assist me with daily routines training for the other employees.

I recommend that the day-to-day users have training for four hours in the morning then immediately deploy the module that afternoon. The next morning when they return to work, their brains have pushed their training into long-term memory and they begin using the system with more confidence. It only gets better for them over the next few days as they practice.

I'd equate learning the new business management system to learning to drive. With an hour of driver's education classes once or twice a week for six weeks, you get good enough to obtain a learner's permit.

Case Study: Learning to Drive

If you were lucky enough when you were fifteen to take driver's education, did you wait around a year or more to get behind the wheel outside of class? I bet you couldn't wait to drive after your first classes even if all you were allowed to do was warm up the car or back it out of the garage. Every short trip to the grocery store, you begged to drive. Then many of us, before we were licensed, were confident they could go it alone.

The first and only joy ride I attempted, the jeep was located on the slightest of inclines in our driveway, and I panicked for forty five minutes struggling with getting it back over its original dry spot after rolling backward thirty feet and killing the motor. Then I flooded the motor in multiple attempts to get back to the original spot.

Spraying the dry spot with the hose didn't occur to this panicked teenager. I knew the dry spot would be blatantly obvious to my extremely sharp-with-the-details father—a cop. That was the day I mastered a clutch. For forty five minutes I practiced and practiced and practiced and finally got the jeep back over its original dry spot. Thank heavens the steam was no longer rolling off the hood when my dad got home. I continued to practice by driving around the pasture with my big brother at my side insuring I didn't hit a cow.

Personnel learning the new business management system are going to be like me with the jeep. They need lots of practice in order to learn. The most expensive cost of training is not doing it or not doing it well. It's like buying a twelve-cylinder Jaguar with a stick shift and giving it to a kid who has never learned to use a clutch on the old jeep. Better the old jeep (the tutorial company) loses its transmission than the Jaguar (the live system).

The employee without adequate training becomes a dangerous employee. One who unknowingly unmarks "Retain History" before closing the module for the year. An employee who prints all 2,400 checks before they get the useful 200 checks they wanted (that happened while I was out to lunch during a client's Go Live). Or the employee who thinks yearend receivables closing didn't work so does it two and three times before calling for technical support. Yearend receivables and payables closing each take seconds to process, and we've had many clients contact us and ask why it isn't working. We've had three or four clients close multiple times before they call.

Or the worst situation, the general ledger accountant who didn't learn to request a backup before starting the yearend general ledger closing. That would have worked out okay except that another employee sat on her mouse while she was out to lunch managing to butt click in just the right spot to repeat yearend closing.

The question is how do you keep the business running and get your personnel trained successfully using low-cost online webinar training? As an executive, how do you support the project? Flying into the training class only at the beginning and end is seagull management. It leaves undesirable results on someone's head.

Conduct training as though you have engaged a professional to do it. Invest in training an internal staff person as a trainer and system manager. It doesn't matter if all they regularly do is collections management. If they have the system aptitude and ability to lead a group of other employees, allocate their time in advance of your Go Live date to come up to speed on the module training so they can lead the balance of your employees through daily routines training.

Along with Chapter I about management support, this list should provide you with insightful tips to increase the value of training you provide to your team. Some tips will be contradictory (like use generic data or develop custom data); use what works for you.

Tip	Comment on the Tip
Schedule and estimate the cost of training with full knowledge	It may take four hours to train customer service personnel, but you won't train all twelve of them at the same time. That fact alone can be a rude realization if you have a tight budget.

Train champions, your stronger personnel; then have them train small groups of other personnel	It not only trains the newer, slower personnel, it's powerful reinforcement of the champion's training.
Nurture your champions	Encourage and incentivize them
Eliminate the interruptions during training	Allow for breaks but insist people get back to class. Start all breaks with this type of statement: "It's 10:05 now; everyone be back in class by 10:20."
Conduct training off site to eliminate interruptions	Use of a cell phone is bad while driving. I know of trainers who won't allow them in the training room
Conduct training for groups of employees appropriate for their jobs	Not everyone needs to review set up options
Support laughter and humor during training	There's nothing like a good laugh to help employees remember the information. It's like the memory trick to associate names with obscure visualizations. Attach a memorable trick to the lesson.
Postpone yearend routines training	Schedule it prior to yearend
Schedule daily routines training the day before you Go Live on that module	Plan Sprint Cycles of training for a half day, implementing the module for the last half of the day. Ten sprints of four-hour training classes are better than forty hours straight of class time. Personnel will retain almost all they learn in four hours because they put it to work immediately. They'll retain less than half of what they learn in forty hours.

Insure your trainer is flexible and skilled enough to meet various learning styles.	People need the training style changed about every fifteen minutes. The trainer reads the book out loud, students read to themselves or out loud, material is demonstrated, hands-on work is inserted between every change of style
Accommodate training needs with good tools	A dedicated room, audio/visual tools, training manuals and materials
Train with training manuals and the training database for the initial training	Investment in creating your own materials is nice, but expensive. The concepts remain the same no matter what the data. The first introduction to the system will be confusing no matter what. The tutorial company and manuals take you through logical steps.
Realize the day after training is always better	Everyone, especially adults, need a good overnight rest for their brains to push what they've learned into long-term memory.
Have Payables and Receivables clerks go through routines training for both modules.	The two modules have so much in common, the extra training provides good reinforcement and sets the stage for cross training and backup
Plan a second round of training three to six months after implementation	You'll be amazed at how much more everyone learns.
If you can afford it, have your trainer develop training videos or manuals with your prototype company data	This is a good tactic for post Go Live training in larger companies or those with high turnover (perhaps their workforce is seasonal). I've had larger clients invest in custom training documents when their situation was relatively unique.
Pair fast learners with slow learners.	Overall it decreases training time and improves the training of the entire team.

Give your fast learners extra hands-on lessons and a break from training slower learners.	You want to keep your champion's interest and support.
Provide incentives for completing training, especially online training.	Keep chocolate, caffeine, and protein snacks handy for employees in training
Don't expect a new employee who used Dynamics GP five years earlier to go without training or be able to implement faster.	They're in the awkward situation of having to unlearn and relearn. In five years, the software has upgraded through two to three versions.
Join a user group and continue learning and teaching tips and tricks	There's nothing like training someone else to reinforce your understanding
Use online training	Online training is good for reinforcement post Go Live and for new employee orientation.
Use online training as primary implementation training only if you assess the drawbacks carefully and accommodate for its needs	Provide a quiet training space, the tutorial company loaded on the same computer (two screens or a large screen are really effective), a printed training manual, and a substantial amount of coffee and chocolate
Use certification tests to insure everyone understand concepts	It helps reinforce the training and points out who needs additional training in various areas. Yes, it's just like grade school testing.
Keep your annual plan current so you have access to free online help communities	Microsoft has over fifty Dynamics GP webinars online in CustomerSource

XVIII. Preparation of Master Records

What you'll learn in this chapter:
- *What constitutes a master record*
- *Alternatives for preparing, cleaning, master records*

Cleaning master records is a common component of nearly all business management system implementations. Master records include but aren't limited to:

- General ledger accounts
- Customers
- Vendors
- Items
- Bills of material
- Employees
- Fixed assets

On the web site www.rapidimplementation.com you'll be able to locate Excel worksheets that provide you with a sample of how a table of master records is formatted. These samples aren't exactly what Dynamics GP uses; like you, we prefer not to have lawyers contact us regarding patent and copyright violations. Therefore, there are numerous other specialized fields for specific business management systems, but these worksheets provide samples for how the various records may be formatted for import.

Alternatives for cleanup of master records, in order of easiest to hardest:

1. Don't clean the data

2. Clean data as you import it—sometimes all you need is a translation table.
3. Clean data between systems in something like Excel, Word, Access, or SQL tables—usually the easiest method.
4. Clean data in the new system—easier than you might think, especially with various Dynamics GP and SQL tools.
5. Clean them in your legacy system—usually very difficult which is why they need cleaning.

Don't-clean Method

If the records are clean, sometimes all that's needed is a mapping during the import. This is relatively fast, easy, and flexible with the RapidStart tool for QuickBooks or Peachtree to Dynamics GP. See Chapter XV The Right Tools are Everything.

Clean-during-import Method

As an example, your old customer data may have customer numbers that are inconsistently formatted. You want to re-identify them and make the identification code length and structure consistent. The Integration Manager can handle this type of change with what's termed a "Translation Table." It looks like this:

ABLECOMPUTER	ABLE0001
COMP	COMP0001
FRIENDLYCOMP	FRIE0001
WESTSIDEELEC	WEST0001
D0234	DOVE0001

Also with Integration Manager, you may run scripts against the data during import. For example, a script might parse the string "Portland, OR 97201" into fields for the city, state, and postal code.

Clean-data-between-systems Method

My favorite tool in the whole world is Microsoft Excel. I'm fairly adept with cleaning data with macros and functions. If you have a lot of data to clean and aren't adept with Excel macros and functions, I highly recommend you find someone who is adept. They will save you a lot of time. Some of the macros and functions that I've found to be most helpful:

Tip	Comment on the Tip
Vlookup or Hlookup	Vertical or horizontal lookup. These functions match data between two tables. If you have addresses in one table and phone numbers in another, you can compile the two into one table if you have a common field in both tables.
CLEAN; CONCATENATE; LEFT, MID, and RIGHT; PROPER; REPLACE, UPPER	These do all kinds of massive functions against the table to help you. For example, all ID's in Dynamics GP are uppercase. So clean the data before you import with one function to change the ID field to all uppercase before import. The Integration Manager can also set all characters to uppercase during import, but sometimes you want to do certain cleanup before the import.
IF, AND, NOT, OR, TRUE	Functions that allow you to look for criteria and change it

If your data exceeds one million lines, then consider Microsoft Access or SQL. Or break your data into manageable sections and use Excel. There's nothing stopping you from importing master records in several steps.

Clean-data-in-new-system Method

This type of cleaning is straightforward when you attach the master records to Classes in Dynamics GP. Customer, Vendor, Item, and Employee

Master Records have classes. Your Customers, for example, could be attached to a Class so that you can change fields such as the payment terms, salesperson ID, or shipping method, in addition to many other fields.

Design of Class records is vital during the design and prototype stages of your implementation. See Chapter XX for more information on set up options, Chapter XVI for RapidStart Tools, and Chapter XII to determine your design and testing during the prototype stage.

In addition, you should consider modifying and combining records in Dynamics GP with the Professional Services Tools Library. See Chapter XV for details on PSTL.

And when nothing else works, SQL Scripts can be written to do almost anything once you've imported legacy data into the Microsoft SQL database.

Clean-data-in-old-system Method

I've never had a client completely successful with this method. It has always required a second pass at the data once we implemented. In situations that stretch out longer, this may be necessary though. Cleaning data before import may be a task well suited for temporary help—those summer interns that I spoke of in Chapter I.

XIX. Importing Historical Data

What you'll learn in this chapter:
- *Options to importing legacy data*
- *Why importing some legacy data is difficult*
- *One of our most complex legacy data imports*

SMBs want to Migrate Historical Data

Most owners and managers of SMBs initially want to translate their legacy payables, receivables, purchase orders, and sales quotes and orders into their new system until I explain how difficult and expensive it can be to import certain types of legacy data. In this chapter I'll discuss the various types of data.

This chapter references Dynamics GP, but much of this information applies to any midmarket business management system. My intention is to present moderately technical material so owners and managers of SMBs take pause at the complexity and begin to fully understand why migrating historical data can become so expensive for them.

General Ledger Historical Data

General ledger transactions are typically the easiest to extract from any type of entry-level or business management software. They're easy to balance, easy to import, and it's quick to prove their integrity. The Dynamics GP Integration Manager tool is free for the first 120 days and easily imports historical general ledger transactions. There are typically only two challenges with legacy general ledger data.

The first challenge involves grouping of general ledger transactions. Some systems may date every single distribution line and group entries by another field—usually the journal entry number or batch ID. With one exception, Dynamics GP groups journal entries by date. The only exception in

Dynamics GP is that a journal entry number can represent two dates: A standard entry and its reversing entry on a subsequent date—the typical accrual and reversing entry at month or yearend. If the journal entry number from the legacy system is significant to the user, we can import it into the transaction or distribution reference field.

The second challenge involves yearend closing processes and entries. Typically the best method is to remove year end closing entries from the legacy data. The Integration Manager imports all general ledger entries into transaction work batches. All fiscal years are originally open, the imported batches are posted, and eventually the historical years are reclosed after proving that the imported transactions balance to the legacy system.

None of the above two challenges are technically difficult.

An SMB can complete a rapid implementation complete with only general ledger beginning balances then import the legacy general ledger entries after the Go Live and before their first yearend closing. Simply insure you identify the beginning balance journal entry and keep the historical fiscal periods open. Once you've closed the historical years, if done correctly, your beginning balance will be double. Reverse the beginning balance journal entry and move ahead.

Payables and Receivables Historical Data

SMBs migrating from entry-level systems may perceive there are only two modules involved. Actually there are at least four modules plus Inventory in most midmarket products.

1. Purchase Order Processing can contain new purchase orders that have had no receiving transactions applied against them, purchase orders with partial or full shipment and/or invoice receipt transactions applied against them, and historical purchase orders completely fulfilled and invoiced. Purchase Order Invoice receiving documents when posted become Payables Transactions.

2. Payables Transactions contain primarily a net amount attached to a distribution of debits and credits with a similar payment transaction of a credit to cash and debit to accounts payable.
3. Sales Order Processing transactions can contain open quotes, orders, returns, and invoices plus historical returns and invoices. These transactions also contain inventory line item information and may have additional complicating factors such as commission distributions, sales taxes, landed costs, separate shipping address per line item, and Analytical Accounting dimensions. Think complex, error-prone, time-consuming integration processes; therefore, expensive. When the invoices in Sales Order Processing are posted they become Receivables transactions.
4. Receivables Transactions contain primarily a net amount attached to a distribution of debits and credits. Cash Receipts within Receivables contain a debit to cash and a credit to accounts receivable.
5. Inventory

Purchase Order Processing

Purchasing transactions include Purchase Orders, Shipment Receipts, and Invoice Receipts matched to the Shipment Receipts—all down to the detail level of line items. A skilled integration specialist can import into the Purchase Order Processing and Payables cycle for all these transaction types. If a client desires the inventory item purchasing history that's easy enough to import open purchase orders. Then it gets tricky matching the shipment and invoice receipts to the Purchase Orders. Since every transaction is imported as a work or open transaction, the import of shipment and invoice receipts must be matched against the open purchase orders; then the purchase orders should be removed to history.

When posted, the Purchase Order Invoice Receipt becomes an open Payables Transaction. Basically the integration import routines are emulating personnel working over a long period of time. There are likely non-inventory receipts in addition to shipment and invoice receipts not matched to a Purchase Order.

Payables

Then we move into the Payables transaction workflow. In addition to the invoices from receiving, there are likely additional invoices posted directly in Payables, plus credit memos, and payments. Historical payables data is spaghetti. Check 1234 pays Invoice A, Invoice B, and half of Invoice C. Then a credit memo is applied against part of the remaining balance of Invoice C. The final amount of Invoice C, plus Invoice D, is paid with check 1345. It's difficult recreating the "apply-to" table—the table that keeps track of what's been paid.

The apply-to records, the records that span the work, open, and history tables of Receivables and Payables, is huge, complex, and not easily created. It's a vital record though—the record that helps you to not pay invoices twice and correctly apply payments and credit memos.

I've found that I can simplify the challenge of creating the apply-to records. The resolution involves determining what's important to the client. Is it important to track each invoice or is it important to track each payment? If an assumption is made that each invoice was paid with one check, I programmatically assign a sequential check number instead of the historical check number to the payment transaction of the invoice. The integration routine will import the invoice into the work file as a paid transaction that will immediately be marked as a historical, fully-paid document with an apply-to record. If I'm able to extract the actual check number that paid the invoice, I'm even better off.

Sales Order Processing

Sales Order Processing (SOP) transactions include:

- Quotes
- Orders and/or Backorders
- Picking Tickets
- Packing Slips
- Returns
- Invoices

SOP transactions include another type of apply-to record—a record that links Quotes, Orders and/or Backorders, and Invoices together. This is in addition to commission, distribution, user-defined field, sales tax, and hold tables. SOP invoices when posted become a Receivables transaction.

Using the same method as above to overcome the challenge presented by the apply-to record, we can apply payments to either the SOP orders or invoices.

Receivables

Receivables transactions are created by the posted SOP returns or invoices. Or receivables transactions can be created as the simpler distribution-type of transaction along with payments. If the historical import process must emulate the actual work process over time, all invoices and debit memos must be imported and posted. Then credit memos are imported, posted, and applied to their appropriate posted invoice. Then payments are imported into work files accompanied by their apply-to record. In Receivables, once every invoice, credit memo, and payment is fully applied, it's processed through monthend closing to move it to the history tables. Recreating this process via integrations is difficult and time-consuming, generally lacking a high degree of accuracy.

Again, to overcome the challenge and somewhat decrease the investment of time necessary to import historical sales records, the integration specialist can create payments against the transactions and import them as paid transaction which can be processed through monthend closing routines to move them to the history tables.

Inventory

Importing inventory history usually isn't completed if SOP invoice history is imported. SOP reports drawn from history tables contain inventory item history. That's the information most SMBs are looking for: what did we sell to whom?

Fixed Assets

Worthy of short mention, the implementation of the Fixed Assets module is usually straightforward. The Integration Manager is typically used. A table of assets is developed as of a point in time, including depreciation-to-date amounts.

Until this month, I've never been involved in an implementation of Fixed Assets when the client desired the detailed depreciation transactions imported into history. This is a special case with a client who self-implemented Fixed Assets and self-upgraded Dynamics GP. We're not sure how, but they completely destroyed the integrity of the asset data tables. We'll be using SSIS (SQL Server Integration Services) to extract, clean, and load the tables.

Payroll and Human Resources

While I know there are consultants who would give me twenty lashes for saying this, if at all possible, outsource your payroll. Correctly computing payroll along with accurately filing and paying payroll taxes, deductions, and benefits is a career. If your company is a professional services company or requires job costing or project accounting involved with labor costs distributions, consider completing payroll internally.

If you're an SMB too small to have a dedicated payroll clerk on staff, your accounting staff will constantly struggle with payroll.

Alternatives to Importing History Transactions

Alternative One

Keep the old software around for a few years. We frequently move the old software onto a standalone workstation or keep it on the old server with restricted access. Easy!

Alternative Two

If the old software or hardware isn't stable, I've printed historical data to PDF files for retention. The data is easy to store, to port around, and sort through. Sometimes I keep the data in custom tables in Microsoft SQL, Access, or Excel—whatever I originally extracted it into.

Other Issues Frequently Encountered while Integrating Historical Data

Clients want to Change the General Ledger Account Structure

The most common complicating factor isn't technically complicated. Clients frequently want to change their chart of accounts structure. I can deal with this change several different ways. Sometimes it's easiest to write a conversion inside of the database tool I'm using to prepare the legacy data: Microsoft SQL, Access, or Excel.

Sometimes a translation table within the Integration Manager is easiest. As the data imports, the table translates the old account number into the new account number.

Old Account	New Account
1000	100-1000-1
1010	100-1010-1
1000A	200-1000-1

Sometimes it's easier to import the data with the legacy account structure and change it using the Professional Services Tools Library (PSTL) Account Modifier and Combiner. PSTL has account combiner and modifier functions that transform general ledger account, vendor ID, customer ID, item ID, and other records. I once had a client I warned, "Don't use this tool too many times. You won't be able to explain or figure out where your data posted initially and where it is now." She used it six times and received a qualified audit opinion that year.

Change Master Records ID's

Similarly, clients want to change their customer, vendor, or item numbers. PSTL makes the new records look like they were the original record. The old number can go away.

I once used the tool twice for one customer in an original edition of it. I found that the account string was identical even though the segment lengths were changing, for example:

100-1010-21-4 equals 10-0101-02-14

So I devised an interim format, moving the old account number to the interim format and then the interim format to the new format:

100-1010-21-4 became 10-20101-302-414, then
10-20101-302-414 became 10-0101-02-14

After doing each modification to the format, account set up must be "check linked" (a GP re-indexing utility), the account format segments viewed and corrected, a system utility processed to reconcile the accounts to the new account format, and, finally, the historical and open years reconciled.

Sounds like a lot, but the tools are all within the system and operate very quickly.

Rapid, Skilled Use of These Tools Keeps your Service Costs Down

The information I'm providing here is just to make you aware of alternatives for consideration so you can make better decisions about the tradeoffs when initially implementing. All of the tools mentioned in this chapter have a great deal more details for use in reference and user manuals.

When I was twenty something, I bought a really cheap, old house. There was a bathtub but no shower; I decided to remodel the bathroom. Periodically I realized I needed a different tool so I would buy it rather than borrow it from my father who was a remodeling contractor (he had resigned from being a cop), but didn't know what I was doing. He seldom came to my house because he always banged his head on the six-foot door jams.

The biggest investment was a huge pipe wrench that I accidentally left leaning against a two-by-four after I nailed up the wallboard. I had a little project of undo then redo, so I still have that huge pipe wrench.

Using the right tool is critical to success and having a dad like mine was like using a consultant as a silver bullet. The kids quickly got tired of running next door to use the toilet for two days while I struggled with reseating our old one. Dad finally came to the rescue and finished my project.

Case Study: A Company and Their Legacy Data Import

Many situations lead to different approaches regarding the import of legacy data during a business management system implementation. This situation taught me a lot about importing and backing up company data.

A long time ago on another planet, a company had been piggy backing on the license of its parent company, a public company with enterprise software on an Amdahl system. Our client only used a tiny fraction of functionality in the enterprise software, but when the software changed ownership, the new software owner provided notice that every company entity using the software would soon owe an annual software license fee. That would mean staggering software licensing costs for functionality my client didn't need.

Our client engaged a consulting firm to perform a needs analysis and request for quote, ultimately ending with the selection of much simpler software. The entire implementation cost would be less than the annual maintenance fees for the enterprise software.

The issue was that over the prior six years, approximately sixty company entities had been owned by my client. In the enterprise software, all company data was in one huge database, segregated only by a company code. I had to figure out a way to extract only the relevant data.

The consultant supporting the enterprise software was peeved at the loss of the revenue and reported back to her software developer that we were not only accessing the data, we had been given permission to access the code. Neither assertion was true, but she was building her case in an attempt to keep the business.

I wasn't monkeying with a small software owner. I was immediately warned that a restraining order would be served on me if my client granted me access to the data, data structure, or code. The restraining order would also involve my new software developer. Neither of the software developer companies involved in this mess were small companies.

My attorney came to the rescue. He suggested I write a simple document explaining what I was and wasn't going to access. He believed non-legal terminology would be better accepted yet he wanted the document to eventually explain what was being done in legal terms, too.

I had made our initial contact with the data only through one of the public company's IT staff person. My document pointed out that only he would extract the data into text files. No data structure would be provided to me. In fact, I would have to guess whether a table contained customers or vendors, transactions or set up information. The data would be provided in what's termed a "normal" format. That means the software code knows what "3" means in the fifth column of the fourteenth table, but I would have no clue. Normal means that the software code understands the data. "De-normalized" means humans can understand the data. Only programmers can come up with the definitions like that.

I explained this in terms all the parties would understand then my attorney reviewed it. He sent the document to all parties.

By that time, "all parties" included two attorneys for the legacy enterprise software developer, two attorneys for the new software developer, two attorneys for the public company, two attorneys for my client company, my attorney, and me. I figured about $400 a minute. I knew the technical aspects, but was kindly advised by my attorney, Mike, to keep my mouth shut unless he granted me permission to speak. That was always the agreement between Mike and I and it always worked well for me.

A telephone conversation was held that lasted about forty-five minutes. Forty-four-and-one-half minutes elapsed with a shouting match between eight attorneys. Finally they all took a breath at the same moment. The leading attorney for the enterprise software said something to the effect, "I have a document explaining a process that's acceptable to us. Who wrote it?"

Upon Mike's cue, I squeaked, "Me."

The attorney polled the others on the line. Everyone agreed it was an acceptable solution. I would have neither access to code nor any clue what the data was that I was expected to translate. Most of it was relatively straightforward except for what that dang "3" meant in one field. Eventually I concluded it meant the address was for a vendor and the vendor was a 1099 vendor.

Eventually, I determined I had 3,400,000 transactions to decipher. I engaged a SQL database engineer for two months to translate the data from text files into custom tables segregated into fifty company databases. A new employee spent two months doing little else but importing the data into company databases.

I spent the two months training and preparing employees to take the main eight companies live by the drop dead date. The other fifty-two companies were historical only with no additional transactions occurring. By the drop dead date, we had to be operative because all the companies we were implementing had to be removed from the enterprise software database. We were successful and on time.

I ended up nearly double over the original estimate which was created to cover setup of six companies. After importing the historical data on the remaining fifty-two companies, the client closed the fiscal years incorrectly. Their IT person failed to keep backups so we had to wipe fifty-two companies clean and reimport the data. Another two months of import work.

Then several more months elapsed and we received a phone call that yet again, the client accounting staff determined that they hadn't closed the companies correctly. Again, the backup hadn't been retained. Another two months of import work.

Two years after the Go Live when we were preparing to upgrade we asked if the imported data had been of value. The client reported that they never had to access the data. They simply needed it if they were audited.

Case Study: Fifty-company Conglomerate with Legacy Payables Data

This company was migrating from Dynamics GP to Dynamics AX. All data in the legacy system was to be removed after one year of allowable migration time. In order to continue to have access to any legacy data, the client determined they needed to migrate all history for both the general ledger and subsidiary modules. General ledger data is generally straightforward.

This integration project lasted a full year. All master records plus all transaction work, open, and historical data were migrated for fifty companies. Modules included general ledger, payables, receivables, bank reconciliation, sales order processing, purchase order processing, inventory, and fixed assets for approximately six years of history.

XX. Rapid Implementation Settings Unique to Microsoft Dynamics® GP

What you'll learn in this chapter:
- *Common self-implementation errors to avoid*
- *Settings that can be simplified for rapid implementations*

Posting Settings

I've seen many small companies with massive problems in their initial use of Dynamics GP because of posting settings.

Some Settings We Simplify

Personnel familiar with QuickBooks, Peachtree, and older legacy accounting systems frequently don't understand the options and flexibility of Dynamics GP. Or they have the best of intentions and pick complex settings purposefully. The settings that I recommend for a rapid start aren't the default settings, but the macro is designed to be run against the initial default settings. If the macro is run against other than the default settings, it may actually set the options opposite of what I regard as the simple settings. I'll post that macro on our site www.rapidimplementation.com, but I caution you to use it at your own risk.

My macro requires the use of batches whenever possible and sets the option to "post through" the general ledger. That's going to cause the posting in the general ledger of most batches to be chained to and immediately followed by the posting of subsidiary module batches. In addition, my macro specifies that transaction dates are used rather than batch dates. That will help keep the subsidiary ledgers in balance with the general ledger most of the time. The macro deselects a lot of the posting reports which frustrate many small company users who have been previously using entry-level products. Entry-level systems generally don't print or even provide posting journals.

Remember the macro is designed to be run against previously untouched posting settings. Run the macro against the Fabrikam company first, post some journals, and evaluate whether you like the settings better.

Posting Beginning Balances

When posting your beginning balances to subsidiary ledgers, posting to the general ledger should be stopped. As soon as you've posted your beginning balances, reset posting to the general ledger.

There are many good training and reference materials regarding how initial beginning balances in subsidiary ledgers should be entered so the amounts don't duplicate posting into general ledger accounts. Those recommended settings are vital and unique to startup. Insure that you pay careful attention to posting settings when you Go Live on your system.

Better Control of Your General Ledger Control Accounts

General Ledger Control Accounts are those that represent the balances of your subsidiary ledgers. The most obvious ones:

- Cash
- Accounts Receivables
- Inventory
- Accounts Payable

As soon as you've posted your beginning balances, not only reset posting to and through the general ledger, open the account cards and unmark Allow Account Entry on your control accounts. General Ledger journal entries made directly to control accounts will typically cause those accounts to become out of balance with their subsidiary ledgers.

Many accountants want to make month and yearend expense accrual and reversing entries to Accounts Payable. I advocate setting up an additional balance sheet liability account specifically for accruals and reversals to insure the control accounts stay in balance and accruals are correctly reversed.

Case Study: Self-reliant Client

With corporate tax filing deadlines on March fifteenth for companies with calendar years, I received a call from a Macintosh Dynamics client late in the afternoon of March fifteenth. The owner was furious his general ledger was empty for the previous calendar year. While they had received some training, they didn't want additional follow-up help and had insisted they had a strong understanding of the system to successfully proceed on their own.

There are a number of settings and actions that can cause the issue they found. Usually we find out there is an issue much sooner than fifteen months into operation; however, this wouldn't be a very interesting book if I only wrote about the typical situations.

With an empty general ledger, most companies don't recover from the typical causes. This client was lucky. The journals were simply un-posted, all 49,000 of them. They filed an extension for their tax return and began using a macro to post 200 batches at a time. The bookkeeper who allowed the problem to happen was discharged.

What was truly unfortunate, in her effort to keep costs down and be self-reliant, the new bookkeeper made the same mistake the next year.

XXI. Document and Forms Formatting

What you'll learn in this chapter:
- *One of our most complex legacy data imports*
- *Why importing some legacy data is difficult*
- *Options to importing legacy data*

We dread upgrading one of our clients every two years because of their PO (purchase order) format. Staffers were accustomed to using Excel templates to produce PO's prior to the implementation of Microsoft Dynamics GP. They continued to want flexible fields on the new PO format. If their description was ninety characters long, they wanted the item description field to expand and other fields to shrink. That's easy in Excel. Not so easy in a relational database.

All system documents and reports isolate data into fields; those fields are assigned specific data types. Within reason, fields can automatically shrink or grow on documents, but the key is, "Within reason." It takes code, data type, and "real estate" (space on the document) to be completely flexible.

A small company writing two invoices or PO's a day can be completely flexible. A company printing 200 PO's a day will forego some flexibility in order to produce the higher volume of invoices.

I see this type of flexibility introduced in all aspects of a small company. In some instances, the small company's flexibility enables it to grow; in other instances, the waste of resources managing the diversity impedes the growth.

In a rapid implementation I recommend prioritization. Do you want document formats exactly like the ones you've previously designed or do you choose to make simple modifications and use the default forms? A simple modification would be to add your company logo. A time-consuming modification involves changing a text report into a graphic report, changing all the fonts in use, and tweaking the size and position of every field. A simple modification can take five minutes. Complex modifications to a single document or report can take twenty hours.

Simple modification: $15.00. Complex modification: $3,000.00.

Graphics on the Forms

One of the more frustrating aspects of designing forms involves drawing vertical lines. Invariably they get tweaked back and forth across the form, creating a space too big or too small, depending upon the information on any particular document.

The recommendation is simple with a rapid implementation. Accept the default forms as they are, add your logo, and get your system implemented quickly. If you must modify your forms, don't request vertical lines.

Formatting Tools

Another advantage of a business management system capable of rapid implementation, it will use Microsoft Word for document formatting. The development template looks and acts very similar to a mail merge document.

Another Twist Involving Document Formats

We recommend to our clients that they advise their customers and vendors of the implementation of the new system and new document formats. A slightly different envelope with a slightly different invoice may not be recognized by your customers and, therefore, may not be timely paid.

We've also had new check formats discarded by vendors. When payment involved discounts, the discounts are usually lost because the customer takes responsibility for the mail not getting through.

When the new business management system changes from postal mail to electronic documents delivered by email or electronic payments transmitted by the bank, I recommend that multiple advance notifications and communications be sent to customers and vendors.

XXII. Rapid Implementation of Financial Statements

What you'll learn in this chapter:
- *Alternatives for initial financial statements*
- *More powerful and flexible tools to use*

For a rapid implementation of Dynamics GP, you can't beat Quick Financials. You can have profit and loss statements and a balance sheet within minutes if you pay attention to key set up functions for general ledger account posting type and categories. Quick Financials position accounts based on general ledger account posting types and categories.

Posting types are either "Balance Sheet" or "Profit and Loss." Categories further classify accounts as Cash, Receivables, Inventory, etc. So the system creates a quick financial statement based on the typical position within a statement.

The category list defaults to 48 categories; while the category name can be changed, the account will be treated by Quick Financials according to its default nature. For example, Cash in position 1 will always be a balance sheet current asset even if you name it Entertainment Expense. You can add categories to the default list, but Quick Financials won't understand how to treat those accounts because you can't define a nature to the account.

So while you can obtain a Quick Financial within minutes, I recommend you invest your learning curve in the more sophisticated and powerful financial statement formatting software products. I'll list some of those products and provide a source for more information about them.

Management Reporter

Microsoft Management Reporter is the replacement product for FRx. FRx was the default financial statement report writer for nearly two decades. Management Reporter uses many of the same concepts and is bundled with the Foundation modules of the Microsoft Dynamics ERP products.

Solver

See this website for details about this product: www.solverusa.com/

Jet Reports

See this website for details about this product: www.jetreports.com/

Implementation Tip

With any financial statement report writer, for a more accurate yet automatic way to make a Statement of Cash Flow I've designed a process to make these statements. Instead of just one account, create two accounts for each category, for example:

- Purchase of Fixed Assets
- Disposal of Fixed Assets
- Long-term liability increase
- Long-term liability decrease
- Common stock, acquisition
- Common stock, disposal

If corrections and adjustments are posted to the appropriate account, when your financial statement definitions calculate the net difference the calculation will be correct.

XXIII. Support for Chicken Feed

What you'll learn in this chapter:
- *Support Alternatives*
- *How to prepare for a support call to minimize the cost*

Policies, procedures, and costs for support should be well understood when you engage with your software developer, reseller, and consultant. I generally define support as training, assistance, and troubleshooting which isn't scheduled more than a week in advance and doesn't exceed eight hours, but it's a fuzzy definition. Developers may provide support direct to both end users and to their resellers and consultants or they may only support their resellers and consultants. Whatever your sources of support, consider these attributes:

- Method of delivery: telephone, web site, email, desktop connection, other methods, or all methods
- Hours of operation based on what time zone
- Response time and whether there's an ability to escalate response time based on severity of the situation
- Ability to escalate if you're not getting the response that you need
- Cost alternatives
- Off-hours policy, along with understanding of cost and response time

When I first started as a Great Plains Software partner in 1990, I evaluated several products on the market. Rob Lloyd, the partner recruiter and manager for Oregon, presented me with several objective source reports prepared annually which documented the evaluation of midmarket business management products. Attributes evaluated included support, technical functionality, ease of use, flexibility, stability, performance, scalability, etc. Great Plains Software always had the highest rating for support; it set the gold standard for software support in the 1990's. And it was almost always in the top three of the other attributes. As a user of accounting software, I believed support was the primary attribute for successful implementation and operation.

I still believe that quality, responsive support is a key to success, and Microsoft offers a number of software maintenance and service support plans to meet your needs. The first year of use of Dynamics, the software maintenance plan is mandatory and includes a small number of support incidents directly with Microsoft Dynamics support. More expensive plans are also available that provide unlimited support within standard support hours, five packs of support to add to the basic software maintenance plans, and a premium support plan if you determine you need support 24/7 for business continuity.

In addition, the definition of a support incident is important to understand the cost. A few examples will help:

1. You could enter a support request entitled, "Difficulty with set up options for Sales Order Processing." You might get lucky and gain assistance for several hours for the cost of one incident. Or the technician may tell you that breakdown of the questions is needed and each will be a separate support incident. I've even heard of the support technicians rejecting involved "support incidents," recommending that you contact your consultant for training.
2. You could enter three support requests:
    a. Assistance with Sales Order Processing sales tax set up
    b. Assistance with Sales Order Processing Invoice set up
    c. Assistance with Sales Order Processing password overrides
3. You could have two quick questions, one on Receivables Cash Receipts and another on Payables Check Processing. Almost certainly the technician will split the questions onto two support incidents.

With the first and second situations, if you truly need assistance with all the settings in Sales Order Processing, you should evaluate whether you want to use one to three support incidents or call your consultant and get charged by the hour. Also evaluate the benefit you would receive if the consultant is familiar with your particular company operations. Sales Order Processing set up is complex and even though the time to explain all the effects of a particular set up option would be covered by the incident, the time your employee spends is valuable. In addition, if the support technician doesn't adequately explore other aspects potentially affected by a change to a set up option, you may have other repercussions.

With the third situation, a short call to your consultant is likely to cost less than a support incident unless you have unlimited support.

Like clients of other successful consulting firms, most of our clients use our support; several supplement our support with either the six support incidents that are combined with the Microsoft Dynamics GP first year plan or with a five pack of support incidents. Because we have network infrastructure staff in addition to Dynamics GP staff, our clients prefer the one-phone-call approach to support in addition to the fact that we're familiar with each company's unique situation.

Software has become more complex, support plans are more complex. I recommend that small and midmarket companies consider all the alternatives for support. A small company with a relatively small list price of software should consider purchasing a Microsoft Dynamics unlimited support plan calculated at twenty-five percent of their list price—an unlimited support plan. For the small client, that's extremely cost effective.

No Support

We encounter what we term orphan clients—those whose original reseller has gone out of business or failed to respond to support requests. Unfortunately, we've had cleanups of implementations when somebody has simply made a bad decision or created a major problem with their business management system. This type of situation is encountered by all good business management system consultants.

My first response is to recognize it's never a one-sided situation. Clients have frequently cut costs by cutting their software maintenance plan, upgrades to software or hardware, or consulting costs, so we approach these situations with caution. There are also hit-and-run resellers—those only interested in the quick sale and large implementation project.

The best recommendation I can make is to go back to Chapter VIII to review the recommendations on selecting a consulting organization. Match your support needs with your reseller's support policy. In all cases, maintaining your software maintenance plan is critical to stable use of your business management system. If you can't afford to maintain your business management system, more seriously consider a hosted system or smaller software product.

Timing

This tip is really basic, but since we encounter it every week, I'm going to provide it. Don't put off the support call until 4:30 p.m. on Friday. At 4:30 p.m. on Friday you have two options: overtime rates or the problem will be solved on Monday. Call for support early in the day and early in the week. Support calls are like the line at the post office. You'll spend less time waiting early in the day and early in the week.

XXIV. Working with Independent Software Vendors

What you'll learn in this chapter:
- *Tips and tricks working with third-party ISVs (Independent Software Vendors)*
- *The various integration methods used by ISVs*

Thousands of ISVs around the globe have chosen Microsoft Dynamics products, especially Dynamics GP, to provide core business management system functionality, allowing the ISV to focus on their specialized niche. The size of the following of ISVs is a strong indicator of what developers think about a product—if they think a product is worthwhile enough to invest their company health, it's a good sign of product viability, structure, and stability for you.

Microsoft Dynamics tools are covered in more detail in Chapter XV, but information about how the tools are used by ISVs follows in this chapter.

eConnect

Data table structure and development tools—especially industry-standard Microsoft development tools—facilitate a symbiotic relationship. ISVs have multiple choices when integrating with Dynamics GP. The most flexible method is through the use of the module eConnect. In layman's language, eConnect allows a hot, live, two-way connection to Microsoft Dynamics GP. Also, eConnect's functionality acts like a virtual user, depending upon the user interface rules of Dynamics GP as it imports and exports data. This control substantially increases the reliability of the data input/output.

Integration Manager

Also heavily used, the Dynamics® GP Integration Manager (GPIM) allows a monitored, one-way data import. Highly flexible with the source of data imported, GPIM reads text, Excel, SQL, and Access data files, plus many others that are accompanied by an ODBC (Open Database Connection).

GPIM can be supplemented with VBA (Visual Basic for Applications) scripts before, during, and after integration. VBA scripts can format the data, modify the data, or delete the file after the import. For example, your data might be in an Excel worksheet with totals and other calculations. For example, the VB script can save the data as results only, removing calculations and totals. It can delete or move the file after a successful import.

GPIM acts like a virtual user when it imports, using all the user interface rules of Dynamics GP. This control substantially increases the reliability of the data import.

For those ISVs that need to pass information into Dynamics GP, the GPIM can be the fastest, easiest, and cheapest way for them to integrate. However, customers are the heaviest users of GPIM, drawing in transactions from custom databases, Excel spreadsheets, and most database formats or desktop applications.

Zap! Integration

Zap! is a Computeration tool described in detail in Chapter XV. We've developed it for several custom database and integration projects and now offer it for clients and developers to use in their situations.

Import Tool

Only use the Import Tool if you are 200% positive you know what you're doing. In other words, don't use the Import Tool!

The Import Tool can access every Dynamics GP table, but you must know the table groups, which table to import into first, and whether or not additional tools like Checklinks or Reconcile are required after the import. The import tool doesn't use data rules. Nothing stops you from importing characters into date or currency fields.

Some field information is normalized. That means normal Dynamics GP code understands the field information; normal people don't understand the data required in the field—that's de-normalized data (go have a beer and figure that one out). For example, "3" in the PM Vendor Master File Vendor Status field means the vendor is temporary.

If you know how to backup your database, have a prototype database with which to test, thoroughly understand the data table rules, and have a significant quantity of data to import into a table not accessible by the Integration Manager or eConnect then consider use of the Import Tool. In other words, don't use the Import Tool!

I personally use the Import Tool is to populate the General Ledger Segment Description Master. My developers use SSIS (SQL Server Integration Services) to integrate straight into the SQL table. The trick with either method is to count the number of times the Segments are used in the Chart of Accounts. Or import the data then run a Checklinks on the Account Master after the import of the Chart of Accounts. The Checklinks will correct the Segment Count Field.

SSIS

SSIS gets the job done when nothing else does. What the Import Tool does, SSIS does for any SQL table.

Case Study: SQL version 7.0 Data Transformation Services

In the late 1990's the integration tool with SQL Server version 7.0 was called DTS (Data Transformation Services). Installations of SQL in the old days more so than in the 21st century, in my experience, could utilize different sort orders or be case sensitive or insensitive when used with eEnterprise (the name of one of the earlier versions of Dynamics GP). However, not all third-party products were compatible with some of the optional SQL sort orders and case settings.

With such a situation at a client who purchased an incompatible third-party product, we had to use DTS to export an entire database into text tables and reimport the database into a new instance of SQL with a fully compatible sort order and case setting. We moved three gigbytes of data in and out in about an hour. DTS was fast and SSIS is even faster.

XXV. Roasted Chicken—Yummy!

What you'll learn in this chapter
- *SSRS Flash Report tips*
- *Features of some ISV products*
- *Integration Manager, Zap! Integration, and the Import Tool*
- *SQL Server Integration Services*

Go Home Early on Friday after Giving your Boss a Flash Report

Accountants have never done their job without a spreadsheet. And most accountants have never had a job where there wasn't a [Flash], [Quick], [Summary], [Friday], [Monday] Report; pick one, whatever you want call it.

The owners and managers of SMBs always want the accountant to bypass the familiar debits and credits and give them a report that quickly tells them the status of the business.

Forget accuracy. You and I know that report was a major headache. It never balanced to the real statements. Sometimes it never balanced, period. And adjustments crept into the real financial statements because they were valid debit and credit memos for payables and receivables. Plus there would be inventory adjustments which affected cost of goods sold or, heaven forbid, a cash adjustment. Personally, I always seemed to overlook an interest charge or deposit error on the Friday Report; my real system balanced to the penny, but I had the extra work of explaining why the Flash Reports differed from the financial statements.

The answer to this headache for my clients has been to develop what we call a "Flash Summary Report" with SSRS (SQL Server Reporting Services). See http://www.computeration.com/integration/. It is deployed on an Intranet (secure, internal web site and available twenty-four hours a day to business owners). It **always** balances and it **always** equals the real financial statements because it **always** gets its data from the real financial accounting system.

In our sample, we detail out the major changes to Cash for the week, the month, and year to date. This can be as simple as reporting a single cash account or you can report multiple checkbooks in multiple company databases. Change the date to get to different weeks; we defined the week as Saturday through Friday. A second portion details changes to Receivables and Payables along with aged Receivables and Payables—exactly like you'll see in GP inquiry windows. Lastly, we went into a balance-sheet-like report, always as of a given day so we choose the Friday date, for the current assets and liabilities. In Phase Two of our report, we provided drilldown to the details comprising the summary balances—all drawn from Dynamics GP tables.

If the Flash Summary Report raises questions, instead of the business owners and managers calling you or making you work late, they double click down into the detail. Now you can go home early on Friday afternoon.

You can do this! It is unbelievably fast to deploy on a Microsoft Dynamics® GP version 10 or 2010 system. Below you'll find a sample of the Flash Summary Report we deploy. Data on the following sample report is from the sample Fabrikam company.

Flash Summary Report

Report Date - 4/12/2017　　Run Date - 6/7/2011 4:11:14 PM　　COMP\wmike

Cash		Week Ending 04/12/2017	MTD	YTD
	Beginning Balance	($568,310)	($564,422)	($378,021)
	Payable Checks		($1,717)	($101,457)
	Net Payroll Checks	($17,309)	($39,197)	($125,858)
	Ending Balance	($605,336)	($605,336)	($605,336)

Receivables		Current Week	MTD	YTD
	Beginning Balance	$1,929,916	$1,978,496	$1,793,654
	Invoiced	$245,977	$245,977	$520,825
	Payments Received	($90,924)	($139,503)	($229,509)
	Credits and Returns		$0	$0
	Ending Balance	$2,084,970	$2,084,970	$2,084,970

Aging of Receivables				
	Current	$269,853		
	0 - 30	$0		
	31 - 60	$10		
	61 and Over	$342		
	Total	$2,084,970		

Payables		Current Week	MTD	YTD
	Beginning Balance	$1,719,402	$1,718,772	$1,706,949
	Invoiced	$328	$1,525	$113,180
	Payments Made	($1,173)	($1,717)	($101,457)
	Credits and Returns	$0	$0	$0
	Misc	$0	$0	$0
	Ending Balance	$1,718,557	$1,718,557	$1,718,557

Aging of Payables				
	Current Period	($21,556)		
	1 - 30 Days	$10,000		
	31 - 60 Days	$288		
	61 and Over	$1,729,825		
	Total	$1,718,557		

Current Assets Summary				
	Cash	($8,321)		
	A/R	$291,672		
	Prepaids			
	WIP			
	Inventory	($128,146)		
	Other	($620)		
	Total Current Assets	$154,585		

Current Liability Summary				
	AP	$42,227		
	Payroll and related liabilities			
	Accrued liabilities	$75,215		
	Current portion of LT debt			
	Other	($27,500)		
	Total Current Liabilities	$89,941		
	Asset value less liabilities	$64,644		

Technical How-to on Deploying a Flash Report based on Live Microsoft Dynamics® GP Data

Our Flash Report started with a generic installation of Microsoft SSRS (SQL Server Reporting Services). As SSRS installation varies for SQL 2005 or 2008, GP 10 or GP 2010, 32-bit or 64-bit, we'll refer you to your Dynamics installation manual for those instructions.

As with any installation before you start, backup your Dynamics code, reports, forms, and both the DYNAMICS system database and company databases. The following tips and procedures aren't for amateurs. You should have a strong understanding of the code structure of Dynamics GP, know how to backup code and data, and know how to utilize SSRS.

Develop in Steps

Break your report into sections. Our Flash Report is actually a compilation of six reports consolidated into a seventh report. We first designed a summary report, ran it for several weeks then deployed the drilldowns. Complete the project in small steps, insuring you are duplicating exactly the same financial results that GP produces.

Obtain Source Projects

For GP version 10.0, for those readers with authorized access, go to CustomerSource to search for "Montego SRS ReportsModels.zip" file and download this file. For GP version 2010, search for SQL Server Reporting Services GP 2010 and download the GP11Reporting.zip. These goodies contain Source Projects for SRS Reports—GP's SQL Stored Procedures used in the SRS reports released within GP 10 and 2010.

The release of Montego, opening up the source projects, implies that we can use any of the GP Stored Procedures for any SSRS report. That goes beyond a Tip to Enlightenment, grasshopper! Always be aware of your legal rights and licensing responsibilities when using tools like Montego.

Find Your Own Sources

We'll use the "Cash" section of our Flash Report for this part of the example. Years back, not being a developer myself, I taught my developer to capture the use of tables and Stored Procedures. For Flash!, for example, we ran the >> Inquiry >> Financial >> Checkbook Balance >> Input your Checkbook ID with a DEXSQL.log turned on. Learn how to turn on a DEXSQL.log by searching Microsoft CustomerSource for "DEXSQL.log."

The art of running a DEXSQL.log involves:

- Activate it in the DEX.INI file
- Open Dynamics GP up to the point where you're ready to run
- the function in GP
- Open Windows Explorer
- Find the DEXSQL.log and delete it
- Return to Dynamics GP and perform the function
- Open Windows Explorer
- Find the DEXSQL.log and rename it (DEXSQL-SAVE.log is
- good)
- Return to Dynamics GP and log out
- Open Windows Explorer
- Find the DEXSQL.log and delete it
- Deactivate the DEXSQL.log in the DEX.INI file

Using Notepad or some similar program, open the DEXSQL-SAVE.log. You'll find that the function calls tables and stored procedures to display the Checkbook Balance. Do your research. The log file isn't clean and easy; you'll need to know what you're looking for. Locate the underlying tables and Stored Procedures you'll want to use in the Cash section of your report.

For the Receivables and Payables sections of the report, we ran the Aged Trial Balance Options. For the Current Assets and Current Liability Summary, we ran the Trial Balance Summary report with a DEXSQL.log file.

Design Documentation

We then documented what initially appeared to be a straightforward little report because we made the common mistake designers and developers frequently make—little things like, "This section is current assets." And initially the developer included all assets. So we slowed down and wrote better specifications:

- A big item – define security access
- What does a week/month/year mean, when does it start, when does it end
- What are current assets and liabilities—accountants know; most developers don't
- Do we include payables computer checks, manual checks, quick checks, and bank reconciliation miscellaneous checks?
- Define the details needed in the drilldown
- Define the custom tables and stored procedure layout

Follow Detailed Technical Processes

I stated this above and it's worth stating again: the following tips and procedures aren't for amateurs. I have deliberately left out detailed instructions for some steps. If you need those, go do your homework first. You should have a strong understanding of the code structure of Dynamics GP, know how to backup code and data, and know how to utilize SSRS and the other tools listed here.

1. SQL 2005 or 2008, 32-bit or 64-bit must be installed
2. Download and unzip the Montego or GP11 reporting zip file (referred to later as *reporting solution)
3. Business Intelligence Development Studio has to be installed – this is the tool used to write SSRS reports
4. From the Business Intelligence Development Studio >>File>>Open>>Project/Solution…/*reporting solution
5. Under the Solution Explorer find GPReports >> Shared Data Sources >> DataSourceGPCompany.rds. Double click on it to open and choose "Edit" to find your SQL Server's connection string.

6. Under the Solution Explorer find GPReports >> Shared Data Sources >> DataSourceGPSystem.rds. Double click on it to open and choose "Edit" to find your SQL Server's connection string.
7. Open your SQL Server Management Server
    a. Create a new (SP) Stored Procedure using the SP in the DEXSQL-SAVE.log as a guideline. You can't use the same SP as it usually won't run correctly and you don't want to be editing the original SP. You can't copy it (licensing rights frown upon this).
    b. Create a SQL Query to run the new SP to insure you're getting the information you want.
    c. After you're satisfied, you're ready to create the SSRS report
8. Return to the Business Intelligence Development Studio, >>
8. Solution Explorer, right click on Reports, select Add New Report
9. Now you're using the Report Wizard. Proceed to write your
9. SSRS report and publish it using GP's standard SSRS reporting process.

Write the Detail Reports

For detailed drilldown reports, write the detail reports the same as the summary report, just remove the script to summarize the information. All of the detail reports retrieve data from the same areas as the corresponding summary reports. The passed-in parameter is used to filter the returned data to the transactions that make up the balance upon which you've chosen to drill down. The current assets and current liabilities summary report allows drill down first into the GL Summary view and then into the GL Detail view.

Setup Account Categories

One additional hint we think is important: many components of the report rely on accurate account categories assigned to general ledger accounts. The client for whom we developed the report used the native categories with several of the names modified.

XXVI. Don't Let the Fox in the Hen House

What you'll learn in this chapter
- *Do's and Don'ts to discourage fraud*
- *Behaviors that might indicate fraud*
- *It's the process, not the system*

The following situations aren't directly related to implementation, but they are related to the operation of a business management system. I find it ironic that frequently the system is blamed when the problem is routed in a faulty process. In one of these cases, the implementation was slightly derailed. In most cases, the implementation of a robust system helped prove the fraud.

Case Study: Don't Sign Blank Checks, Ever!

My first encounter with fraud was when I was called in by an owner I'd never met who quizzed me about:

- My involvement with his initial implementation—none
- Support services I had provided to his bookkeeper—one-half-hour meeting
- What I knew about company operations—nothing
- How well I knew his bookkeeper—barely

This incident was my first encounter with fraud, and I had no clue what the problem was. By nature, I'm an extremely poor poker player because I simply cannot lie, deceive, or bluff. I passed the small company owner's quiz.

Then he told me that several years ago he had gone on vacation and signed six blank checks before he left. At that point, I read between the lines and knew why I had been questioned. The blank checks were easy for him and easy for her. Gradually over time, every bill was paid with a presigned check. Gradually over time, the bills got paid with one check for the vendor and one check for the bookkeeper.

The bookkeeper's husband retired; he and his wife were living comfortably with the salary and bonuses his wife was earning. They remodeled their house, bought themselves a new SUV, bought a new SUV for their daughter, and had short but memorable vacations.

Over six years the bookkeeper had gotten to a point where expenses were double and the owner hadn't noticed. He got suspicious though when he found he had no key to the bookkeeper's office and he thought he should be more profitable.

Case Study: Don't Get Stuck in the Denial Phase

My second encounter began with suspicions followed by a little research while chatting with one of my clients. He had recently departed an international CPA firm where he had specialized in forensic accounting. I asked him how he detected fraud, and he told me these were the telltale signs:

1. Gut feel
2. Chaos
3. Defensiveness
4. Failure to take vacations
5. Suspicion of drugs or gambling
6. Inappropriate lifestyle in comparison to the wages
7. Owners have provided too much opportunity
8. Anytime there's cash involved

In a majority of fraud cases, the owners' or managers' first feeling is one of denial and continues through several stages similar to the stages of grief.

I presented my findings "up the chain of command" to a senior manager. He immediately went into denial, and over a few weeks, his feelings didn't move to a second or subsequent stage. I simply withdrew from the implementation. Six months later, their situation was public news and the manager was in a lot of trouble for ignoring the situation.

Case Study: Trust Your Gut

In this situation, the controller with a firm provided little notice when she resigned. In desperation, they hired the first applicant and put him to work the same day of the first interview. I was coincidentally at the office at that time and witnessed his first transaction, a cash receipt. In this particular industry, receipt of cash was a daily occurrence. New clients usually pay for the first appointment in cash.

The new bookkeeper was obsessed about the cash laid on his desk. He couldn't leave it alone; he put it in the safe, took it out and put it in a drawer, put it in an inbox in a file folder, moved it to a file drawer.... Knowing the prior controller's standard procedures, I gave the new bookkeeper some guidance, but made a mental note I thought there was a problem. With this third experience I finally knew to trust my gut. I advised a manager of my concerns, but he wasn't very receptive to the warning.

On the next contact with my client, I was advised that a background investigation of the bookkeeper revealed he was a twice convicted felon for fraud and on probation. One of the terms of the probation included the requirement that he not accept work dealing with money. Not a surprise.

I was tasked with preventing the bookkeeper from stealing from the firm while they found someone else. I advised the managing partner there was no way I could do that, but I could set up a process to determine how much he stole. We advised all the partners to give all checks and cash to the receptionist to photocopy before giving them to the bookkeeper. In thirty days when the firm finally hired a replacement, we determined that no cash had been deposited during the employment term of the felon. Between the office and the bank, a new deposit slip had been written out any time cash was involved. In the five weeks of employment, he had stolen about $7,000 in cash to support his drug habit.

The firm never recovered any of the stolen funds; the bookkeeper returned to prison for parole violation and lost permanent custody of his eight year old son. He was a brilliant man with impressive writing and analytical skills, having written a process improvement analysis that was highly beneficial to the company.

Case Study: It's Not Brain Surgery

Yes folks, I've written most of the book waiting until I could write this: It's neither brain surgery nor rocket science to prevent fraud.

So the next case was settled "on the court house steps." I was contacted by a bookkeeper I hadn't worked with before. She worked in a glass office recently constructed in view of all the entrances to the examination rooms for two neurosurgeons.

The bookkeeper wouldn't allow me to log onto the system. She simply quizzed me with technical questions. Okay, fine, I really didn't want to know what the going rate for brain surgery was at the time. I wasn't suspicious of her because the defensiveness was appropriate. The office was immaculate and orderly and a two-week vacation was planned.

Then I got a nasty call from an assistant district attorney. Seems the vacation was courtesy of the doctors who were getting suspicious and had contacted their CPA. While the bookkeeper was gone, the doctors intercepted her mail and phone calls–the ones about the electricity being turned off and the doors being locked if the bills weren't soon paid.

They fired her and then remembered their patient histories and prior year accounting archives were stored in fireproof filing cabinets at her farm. They arrived at the farm in time to see the bonfire in the middle of a field.

These guys didn't mess around. They filed both criminal and civil charges, and I was a primary target of several attorneys to determine what I knew.

Eventually the attorneys and doctors calmed down and allowed me to help them access the system; the system for which they had failed to obtain passwords. We found two sets of company databases–the real ones which showed that the doctors were bankrupt and the other one used to prepare financial statements.

The settlement was reached minutes before the criminal court trial convened. I received a whopping $7.00 check as an expert witness, but was advised not to cash it because the case didn't go to court. I had provided a substantial number of hours assisting in the case with no compensation and didn't want to get further involved so I withdrew.

Case Study: The Lifestyle Didn't Match the Compensation

One of the cases of fraud I encountered left me extremely frustrated. A bookkeeper was fired and we were engaged by a small out-of-state agency. Their hardware and software were badly obsolete; before we would agree to examine the system we insisted that it be upgraded and stabilized.

I engaged a CPA on contract to reconcile the accounts receivable. On one of her first visits on site, she was approached over the lunch hour by a gentleman paying his monthly sixty-four dollar charge. He brazenly asked if she would honor the same arrangement as the prior bookkeeper. Being a quick thinker, she instantly agreed. He handed her sixty dollars in cash and wished her a good day.

We immediately dove into the bank reconciliation and noted that little cash was ever deposited. No cash receipt in Dynamics GP was ever posted against an accounts receivable account; only credit memos were applied to the accounts with notations about payments.

Taking this information to the general manager of the agency, he went into deep denial initially. In a few days I was called on site for a meeting with the advisory council. I didn't know until I walked into the meeting room that half the town was there including a local newspaper reporter. The next day, my attorney called me and asked, "What have you gotten into now?"

Inside of thirty days, the general manager wanted six years of reconciling work done so the attorney could go after the accounts. Unable to meet their expectations with the mountain of data to review and six years of input to recreate, we had to withdraw from the engagement. I doubt they ever recovered a dime. The math is: 800 accounts times 72 months times $4 per month = $230,400. We understand the bookkeeper owned some really nice purebred cattle.

A surprising circumstance to me is that the municipality passed its audit every year. I know audits don't cover fraud, but someone should have noticed credit memo instead of cash receipt transaction types were being entered.

Case Study: Homeland Security Got Involved

A very recent case involved the acquisition of a new remote sales location for a well-established business of over fifty years. The president thought the new location sales were really great with seven $30,000 to $40,000 electronic devices sold in the last few months.

He learned otherwise when he was contacted by Homeland Security once they detected that the devices were being shipped to third-world countries without proper export documentation. We implemented just in time to demonstrate that the cost of sales for the new location was totally out of line with the revenue.

Case Study: Whiteout

- Uninvolved owner
- Too much authority granted by the owner who was about to sell the business and retire
- Books "didn't quite make sense" – the first reaction was "that d*&% software…."
- I was given a copy of the incorrect financial statements and noticed the shadow of a glob of whiteout on the photocopy
- As soon as I added up the balance sheet, I realized someone had whited out the leading "$1," on the inventory balance, changing it from $1,300,000 to just 300,000.
- I actually located the original document in a desk drawer with the glob of whiteout
- The sale fell through. The owner lost all the equity and goodwill of his company and simply closed the doors.

Case Study: Too Many Crises

I encountered a woman in the 1990's who seemed extremely competent. Despite making arrangements for a follow-up meeting to discuss partnership, she disappeared for several years. Several times when I would later encounter her, there was always a similar period of lapsed time explained by back surgery, a parent's death, an emergency appendectomy.... After each of these meetings, I always expressed my sympathy and noted she seemed to have a lot of these problems.

Then she was hired at a client, and I thought that was great stability for her and competency for the client. They weren't the greatest of clients. They only paid me for the last visit the next time they needed me. I finally became impatient with them and asked for payment for the last visit plus a two-hour prepayment. They sent the funds; I sent the portion for the prepayment back and wrote them that they needed to find someone else.

Several months later the bookkeeper contacted me for a job. We met several times over two days then she disappeared again. Two months later, I received a call in the early evening and she asked to come to my house to talk. Finally by 10:00 p.m., I asked her to leave.

She dropped to the floor and began praying then explained that she was a repeated embezzler who had just been caught by her employer. She was afraid to go home, expecting that the police would be waiting for her. Her husband knew nothing about her drug and gambling addiction. This time in addition to the theft of funds, she asserted she had $75,000 in credit card debt.

Case Study: It Can Happen to Anyone

This case was downright scary to me. It was fraud committed on my business checking account. I caught it very quickly when I viewed my account online and noted three checks for the same amount that I didn't remember writing. The check numbers were completely different from my checks. I called the bank immediately and we closed the account.

The next day I viewed the account online again and noted a fourth check for the exact amount: $57. I again called the bank and the representative said, "You don't even want to know the pending transactions I can see. The first checks were just testing the account."

Two weeks later, a fellow showed up at my office and introduced himself as an investigator. He asked a whole lot of questions including, "Do you have access to blank check stock." I openly showed him the portfolios we provided to new clients to assist them with document formats for checks, invoices, purchases orders, and envelopes.

Then he asked me if I had been at the bank on a particular day in the early afternoon. I looked up my deposit receipts and said, "No. I only go to the bank to make deposits and I wasn't there on that day." Dang good thing!

He then showed me a picture of the bank lobby with a lady at the teller window that was a dead ringer for me from the back; same height, weight, and hair. The lady was cashing one of the fraudulent checks drawn on my account. I had to sit down and could hardly speak. He rapidly assured me he could tell I wasn't the thief. He was actually a police detective. We spent considerable time reviewing the blank check stock I had, discussing the checks which I had received from the closed account, analyzing the handwriting from a novice viewpoint, and noting the names used for the check recipient, signer, and endorser. Six months later, the detective was able to solve the case and put a major check kiting group out of business.

Summary

- Don't provide the opportunity for fraud by giving out too much authority. This is a broad statement that covers check signing, making deposits, purchasing, providing company credit cards, etc.
- Divide responsibilities whenever possible. Someone with no bookkeeping responsibilities should open the mail and receive all payments. The bookkeeper is there to record the information. Someone else should take the deposit to the bank, especially if it contains cash.
- Have your bank statement delivered to your home and reconcile it to receipts and disbursements monthly.
- Small businesses have no business providing high limit corporate credit cards. Control your potential for loss by setting a nominal credit limit.
- Unexpectedly throughout the year, have your CPA review a month of transactions, especially payments and cash receipts.
- Insure your bookkeeper takes a two-week vacation every year and put a temp in charge for that time. Your CPA can usually assist you with putting one of their staff on your site for the two weeks.
- Engage a bookkeeper that's organized and orderly with their work. Chaos can cover up a lot of fraud. If they're a good bookkeeper,

their office and records will reflect their need for organization and attention to detail.
- Get suspicious of defensiveness. It's your right to ask questions.
- For less than $100 you can have all new employees undergo a drug and background check. Talk to your attorney about insuring your policies are in place to do so legally.
- Listen to your gut.
- Look for the signs of unreasonable behavior
- Insure that transactions are appropriate—cash receipts not credit memos, for example.
- If you have online access to your bank account, check and reconcile to your system regularly

XXVII. Move Away from Custom Core Systems

What you'll learn in this chapter
- *My opinion about custom software for basic accounting*

Business solution software is of two major types: horizontal solutions which fit the financial core of nearly all businesses or vertical solutions designed to fit industry-specific requirements.

Vertical solutions are initially created by software programmers when somebody does business so uniquely that only a specialized program will meet their needs. Then the programmer expands their customer base by expanding their sales to additional clients in the same industry.

The situation goes awry when the programmer writes core financial modules instead of linking the vertical solution to existing financial modules from the wealth of horizontal solutions with strong integration tools. In my viewpoint, double-entry accounting hasn't changed for over 500 years and for good reason–it works. The vertical solution developers shouldn't be writing custom core modules.

At the core of nearly every business I have encountered since I took bookkeeping class as a sophomore in high school, everyone pays bills the same way, everyone has a general ledger as the basis for financial reporting and budgeting, and all companies have a source of income, typically customers, sometimes grants or trusts. Core modules cover the basics for accounting for employees, assets, inventory, bank reconciliation, and debts.

It is a far better practice to buy industry-standard software for as many core functions as possible; then add a vertical software product. Most of the big business management software developers are using industry-standard tools and databases which make the integration of vertical software modules and core modules nearly seamless.

Custom systems are the solutions that industry-standard packages replace most often because of these common problems:

- The small, custom developer simply can't keep up. They get bogged down in their niche with user change requests and never complete development of the core financial, payables, or receivables products.
- The small, custom developer gets bogged down with support.
- The small, custom developer can't keep up with technology while competition is moving to an Internet-based, collaborative environment.
- Custom vendors seldom provide advanced modules such as Collection Management or Collaborative Demand Planner that you may want to add.
- Integration procedures for imported and exported data are weak in the custom product, especially as technology advances.
- The cost of development of the product is spread over a much smaller user base, generally making the product more expensive.
- The support and implementation channel of a custom vendor is weak and shallow, usually geographically limited. Installation and training expenses are generally higher than with industry-standard packages.
- If the developer of a custom package goes out of business, you start over.
- To protect yourself from the potential of the custom developer going out of business, it's a wise idea to have source code put into escrow, adding another annual cost to your software.
- With a smaller base of customers and installations, custom software requires more intense prototyping and testing before live deployment, increasing your costs even more.

There are about a dozen custom solution software packages that have measurable market share. Their technology lags behind the industry giants, but they are well established and viable. I personally think they should take what's unique and link it to the core financial modules of the industry giants, but I haven't been in the conference rooms when that issue was negotiated.

XXVIII. A Rotten Egg

What you'll read in this chapter
- *Priceless case studies of what not to do*

Case Study: Loss of Key Employees

I began the implementation of a minicomputer system in the 1980's with the executive oversight provided by the owner's neighbor, a retired executive from IBM. I mentioned this earlier in the book; the first problem was that the fellow wouldn't keep his hand off my leg. That was cured during a management dinner one evening with spouses present when I simply loudly told him to remove his hand from my leg.

Otherwise, he was an excellent project manager who taught me to maintain a very simple, columnar task/action/issue list. The cardinal rule of this type of list is to keep it simple. No large blocks of information or comments, no links. A sample of my current version is on www.rapidimplementation.com.

The failure of this implementation came shortly after my first anniversary on the job. I finally chased down a $38,000 accounting entry causing my accounts payable to be out of balance with its control account. The entry came from an omitted reversing entry from the year prior to my employment. The CPA had made the accrual entry for tax purposes on December 31st, but never reversed it January 1st of the next year.

Along with that entry I located approximately $1,500,000 of entries for a capital expense construction project that had been allocated to the cost of goods sold. The impact of that entry caused the internal union production people to lose their profit sharing contribution the prior year because their contract called for a calculation based on gross profit margin.

Shortly afterwards, I witnessed what I regarded as an unacceptable illegal action by several employees under direction of a vice president, a close friend of the owner. He was quite surprised to see me in the warehouse at that moment.

Before I could complete the implementation, I sweated out a 90 minute interrogation by the owner pressuring me to confess to embezzling the $38,000. I presented him with my issues with his company and he chose to fire me. Charges against me were never brought and I collected unemployment for about two months uncontested. However, about six months later, he sold the company after the IRS and EPA inspections.

Business management system implementations frequently fail when there is turnover of key personnel during the implementation.

Case Study: Culture War I

I was marginally involved with two implementations that both failed due to what I call culture wars.

I began an implementation working with the controller and sales manager of a satellite office of a multinational corporation. The controller took a prescheduled vacation week shortly after we started discovery. He urged me and the sales manager to continue meeting regarding inventory and sales discovery.

We made great progress and were able to move into prototyping set up options in the inventory and sales modules. However, when the controller returned, he was furious at our progress and dismissed me from the implementation. He shortly lost his job though.

The new controller continued to use another implementer, but the sales manager again called me in for consultation. When he met me in the parking lot and ushered me through a back door to the cafeteria for our meeting, I knew there were still major power struggles. I declined to engage with the project.

Years later the controller befriended me and explained that he and the sales manager reported to financial and sales managers at headquarters. The power struggle between them went all the way to the top management of the company.

Case Study: Culture War II

I was on my way to the kickoff meeting for an installation when I stopped at a sandwich shop near the client's office for lunch. I hadn't met any of the personnel on this project several states away from me because I had just been asked to engage as a subject matter expert. Two men in line in front of me were discussing a female coworker. She reported to one of the men and managed the other. Their conversation was rather blatantly discriminatory. The two men were trying to force the woman out of her position so the one fellow could advance.

Thirty minutes later, I encountered both men and the woman at the implementation kick off meeting. One of the men recognized me and did his best to melt into the floor.

Because I was deeply involved in another implementation, I backed out of this implementation. Approximately a year later I learned of its failure.

If your company has culture wars or power struggles going on, deal with those problems. Don't start an implementation and hope for the best.

Case Study: Not Using Your System is a Failure

We have had several clients over the years that use their systems like fancy typewriters. Sales invoices are manually prepared then simply retyped into the system to record the sale. Inventory isn't implemented or the majority of items aren't set up in the system. A former client purchased the fixed asset module in 1998 and had not yet implemented it by the time they were acquired in 2012.

We engaged with a client shortly after Y2K who had purchased Dynamics GP from another reseller, but failed to implement. In 2012 we discouraged them from renewing their annual plan because they had yet to implement the software after ten years.

I engaged with an existing client in the 1990's who had purchased a forty-five-user license from their previous reseller. He had convinced them that they needed the licenses because they had forty-five employees. When I renewed their annual software maintenance plan for only the three accounting users and recommended they drop the other forty-two-user user licenses, the owner cried.

Two days before sending this book to the publisher we met a small client who stated they owned every module of Dynamics GP Advanced Management and several integrated ISV products—software licenses totaling well over $100,000. They use general ledger, payables, receivables, and bank reconciliation.

I'll close here with a pleading to please do your homework.

About the Author

I began my accounting career as a bookkeeping student in my sophomore year of high school. My conservative father didn't believe in borrowing money, plus he was in and out of the veteran's hospital when I was a senior. I was accepted to both Georgetown University and Whitman College, but because of my father's health, I declined the scholarships and student loans. I moved into my own apartment on my eighteenth birthday and started working downtown Portland at a tire company while attending night classes at Clark College in Vancouver, WA.

A year later while my husband was in Vietnam, I attended Oregon State University for a year. Two kids and a divorce later, I attended Solano Community College in central California in order to finally obtain my AA degree before moving back to Portland.

I got my start with system implementations in 1979 at a local division of a propane company owned by a Fortune 100 company. My boss explained to me on my first day at work while touring the facilities that she intended to have more electricity brought in the next day to the computer room in order to increase the response time of two IBM System 34's. I cautioned her against that as respectfully as I could.

I moved on from there to a small company with $1,000,000 in annual revenue. The owners wanted the accounting on the network so they could view individual transactions. They were software developers for Digital Equipment Company (DEC) minicomputer sort and Pascal compiler programs. It was at that company where I first encountered the dreaded Friday report.

When the developers started a new version of compiler, I received the old minicomputer. Each month before I closed payables and receivables distributions to the general ledger, I had to beg for disk space. I needed one to two megabytes. I didn't always get what I needed; the program would crash during closing. I would have to restore and reimplement the software, determine what had posted to the general ledger and what didn't; why transactions from two and three months back would repost in some months.

I left that company in December 1983 to complete my business administration degree and obtain my CMA (Certified Management Accountant) designation. At my going-away party, I remember answering the question about what I wanted to do next: "I don't know exactly, but I do know I never want to implement another accounting system in my life."

Since then, I've never worked doing anything else. From August 1984 to late 1989 I worked at a variety of midsize companies implementing minicomputer systems.

I realized I was good at implementing systems in 1989, so I signed up as a Great Plains Software reseller. By 2001, I was the reseller of record for 125 Great Plains Software DOS or Macintosh systems—most of which I had installed by myself. While I had five employees in early 1992, I closed the business down for several months to work for one client before I again started up on my own the first of 1993.

In 1992, I was the only woman who participated at the reseller meeting following the Great Plains Stampede. I understand I was the first woman invited to that post-Stampede meeting. There were about twenty resellers in the meeting surrounded by about thirty Great Plains personnel. We weren't told what we were doing, but it was evident we were providing input to a new product. In March of 1993, Great Plains Dynamics was announced.

I've lost track now of the number of installations I've completed. I marvel at how each differs, yet at what they have in common. There have been many twists and events over the years, but Great Plains Software and Dynamics by any name has been at the heart of my work since 1989.

My escape from implementations is to visit National Parks and my typical souvenir is a piece of pottery. My cover art is homage to a thirty-inch-high ceramic chicken entitled Dorian Moon. I acquired her on such a trip when a large implementation was delayed. I learned I had thirty days of grace at 2:20 p.m. and was on a plane to Kalispell, Montana by 5:30 p.m. I cruised Glacier National Park in a red mustang convertible. The next morning I had two margaritas by noon and wisely decided to walk into town. Wandering into an art gallery, the young woman who met me asked what I was looking for. In my light-hearted mood, I said to her, "Something I can't live without." She was a little put off and let me wander on my own.

I had missed a charity event the night before; everything I saw that I liked was already sold. As I was leaving, I remarked to the young lady how much I liked the ceramic chickens, but lamented that they were all sold. She told me she thought the best chicken had been overlooked because it was in the front window. As soon as I saw her, I instantly knew I couldn't live another day without owning Dorian Moon. However, my concern even with two margarita's affecting me was how I would get the chicken back to Portland. The clerk called the artist who assured me he would pack her well.

Several weeks later I was contacted by the trucking company who brought Dorian Moon to Portland. I was advised I had to pick her up at 4:00 p.m. during the shift change. When I stepped up to the counter, the woman stared at me for a long moment then announced on the microphone, "Rooster, the chicken lady is here."

The entire company came to the office which is why they asked me to show up at the shift change. I'm not sure who they expected to see. I'm a relatively normal-looking woman. Everyone at the plant was able to view Dorian through a window the artist had cut in the cardboard. He had written a note on the box that carefully explained she needed to see out of the window during her trip.

I have no idea if they nicknamed Dorian's driver Rooster just because he had driven the truck or if that was a previous nickname. Some things are better left unquestioned. He brought Dorian to my car with a forklift. She had been suspended using foam straps glued together with duct tape—hundreds of yards of duct tape—in a huge crate built from used wooden pallets. Rooster assured me she had an excellent view the entire trip.

The system went live a month late and the client remains a great client to this day.